Murder on a Starry Night

A Queen Bees Quilt Mystery

by
Sally Goldenbaum

Other Queen Bees mysteries by Sally Goldenbaum:

Murders on Elderberry Road **(2003)**
A Murder of Taste **(2004)**

Murder on a Starry Night
A Queen Bees Quilt Mystery

By Sally Goldenbaum

Editor: Doug Weaver
Cover illustration and map: Neil Nakahodo
Character illustrations: Lon Eric Craven
Design: Vicky Frenkel

Published by Kansas City Star Books.

First edition.

ISBN 10: 1-933466-07-3
ISBN 13: 978-1-933466-07-1

Printed in the United States of America by Walsworth Publishing Co.,
Marceline, Missouri

To order copies, call StarInfo at (816) 234-4636 and say "BOOI

Order on-line at www.TheKansasCityStore.com.

**STAR
BOOKS**

Murder on a Starry Night

A Queen Bees Quilt Mystery

by
Sally Goldenbaum

KANSAS CITY STAR BOOKS

STAR
BOOKS

CAST OF CHARACTERS

PORTIA (PO) PALTROW,
founder and nurturer of the
Queen Bees quilting group.
Anchors the women's quilting
group in life and in art.

KATE SIMPSON,
Po's goddaughter and
a high school teacher.
The newest member
of the Queen Bees.

PHOEBE MELLON,
wife to Jimmy, an up-and-
coming lawyer, young mother
to eleven-month-old twins,
and a constant surprise to
her quilting cohorts.

ELEANOR CANTERBURY,
who lives on the edge of the
college her great-grandfa-
ther founded. Is heir to the
Canterbury family fortune.

LEAH SARANDON,
professor of women's
studies at Canterbury
College. An artistic
quilter.

SELMA PARKER,
owner of Parker's Dry Goods
Store. Provides a weekly
gathering place for the
Queen Bees quilting group
and generous doses of
down-home wisdom.

SUSAN MILLER,
Selma's artistic assistant
manager in the quilt
shop. Recently returned
to college to pursue a
degree in fiber arts.

MAGGIE HELMERS,
Crestwood's favorite vete-
rinarian. Is an avid quilter
and collector of fat lady art.

M A P

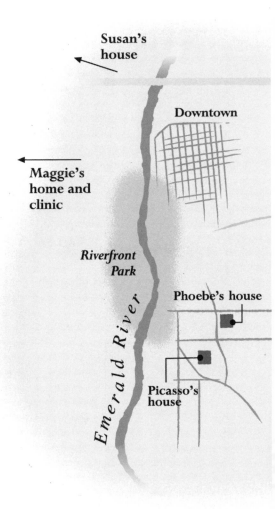

Susan's house

Downtown

Maggie's home and clinic

Riverfront Park

Phoebe's house

Emerald River

Picasso's house

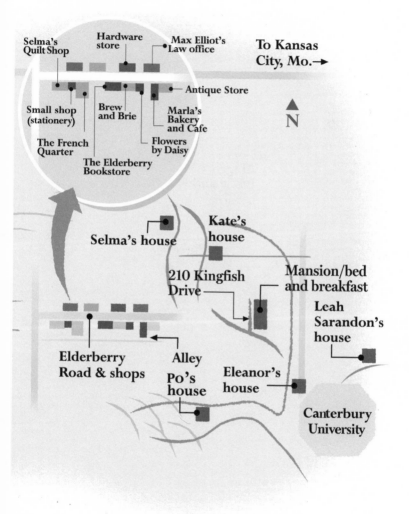

Selma's Quilt Shop

Hardware store

Max Elliot's Law office

To Kansas City, Mo. →

N

Antique Store

Small shop (stationery)

Brew and Brie

Marla's Bakery and Cafe

The French Quarter

Flowers by Daisy

The Elderberry Bookstore

Selma's house

Kate's house

210 Kingfish Drive

Mansion/bed and breakfast

Leah Sarandon's house

Elderberry Road & shops

Alley

Po's house

Eleanor's house

Canterbury University

PRELUDE

Oliver Harrington II walked down the back staircase from his second-floor bedroom, one hand gripping the banister tightly.

The noises had come from the kitchen, Ollie thought. He wasn't afraid, really. Things made him anxious sometimes, but not really afraid. In fact, Ollie couldn't remember ever being afraid in all his fifty-two years. He didn't get angry much, either. Hardly ever. But he was angry this time, more angry than he had ever been in his whole life. Because it wasn't fair. None of it. That's probably why he was hearing things—hearing the uncomfortable anger rattling around in his head.

Narrow windows along the side of the staircase looked out over the lawns and gardens of the Harrington Estate. But Oliver's eyes didn't see the lawns and gardens; immediately, almost as if beyond his control, they looked upward toward the heavens.

It was a deep, starry night, and Ollie could see the great Andromeda Galaxy with his naked eye. He paused on the staircase, his breath catching in his throat. Exquisite. Miraculous. Nearly 3 million light years away, and he could see it from this window of his home in Crestwood, Kansas. It was surely a miracle.

Finally, Ollie forced himself to breathe, but the dazzling beauty of the universe above him was almost more than he could handle. For as long as Ollie could remember, this was where he was the most comfortable — looking up into the universe and learning every single thing he could about how it worked. And the amazement he felt never dimmed, just like the North Star.

"Glorious," he said and the single word traveled out of his mouth and pierced the still, predawn air, echoing down the hardwood stairs before him.

When Oliver was a boy, the back staircase had been the way servants got to the kitchen quickly and silently from their third floor rooms. He couldn't remember when that had changed. Probably when he and his twin sister Adele were college age and Adele went off to her east coast school, but he couldn't be sure.

Oliver had lived in the Harrington mansion nearly his whole life. He'd left briefly for junior college in the east, a school his mother chose carefully, one that would afford him attention and a chance to explore the things he loved — astronomy, writing. It hadn't worked, though. They made him take other subjects that didn't capture his mind and spirit, and Oliver failed. So after a year, Oliver came back home. And years later, he finally got the degree that would have so pleased his mother, a bachelors in science from Canterbury College. Or university as they wanted to call it now, though it seemed a little uppity to Ollie. And then the professors had let him stay on, taking any classes he wanted to take.

A bang beneath him halted Oliver's body on the bottom step. Was there someone in the house? He could feel something nearby.

Probably some neighborhood kid playing a trick on me, Oliver thought. Maybe he should start locking his doors—his friend Halley had been surprised when she discovered he didn't lock up. But she didn't grow up in a small town—she didn't understand. *Halley worried about too many things*, he thought —wills and deeds and things that didn't matter much to Oliver. Other people worried about those things, too, but Ollie just smiled and agreed, and that seemed to make everyone feel better.

His clear brown eyes fought the fog of darkness in front of him. Finally his bare feet felt the flat smooth surface of the floor and he moved to the wall, flicking on the light switch.

Yellow light fell on the wide planked flooring and bounced off the stainless steel counter and refrigerator. The kitchen was big enough to feed an army, Halley had told him the other day, but Oliver kept every surface clean and sparkling. He loved the stainless tops because you could see the perfect shiny surface, clear of even a thumbprint or a smudge. Oliver loved its orderliness, the pots hanging in order of size, the cups in the glass-fronted cabinets lined up in perfect symmetry. Oliver loved this house. It was way too big for him, he knew that, and all sorts of people were telling him that these days. *Move to a small condo, Ollie,* Tom Adler kept telling him. *I'll find you the best in the city and take this monster off your hands.* But 210 Kingfish Drive wasn't a monster at all. It was home. Always would be.

Ollie looked around the room and out across the wooded back yard, back toward the pond that Joe, his gardener, tended to. No branches moved in the Indian summer night. No sound. Only the silence of the stars. Silly. No one was here. Just in his dreams, that's all.

Oliver pressed the boiling water button on his sink and filled a china cup with the liquid, then scooped up a cup of loose herbed tea from the canister on the counter. He and Halley and Joe had laughed about that the other day—how Ollie made midnight trips to the kitchen for a cup of tea. They didn't believe him that herbed tea solved all ills. But it was true. He'd sleep like a baby tonight. A cup of ginger tea and the fog in his head would clear. He was being silly. Hearing things.

His eyes slowly adjusted to the light and he looked around the spacious room, took in the wide island in the center of the room, the door leading out to a small enclosed porch where years ago the milkman left bottles of fresh milk and the Harrington twins lined up their boots after building snowmen in the backyard. The door to the porch was slightly ajar. Oliver frowned. Had he left it open when he let his cat back in the house before going to bed? He reached out and closed it with the flat of his hand, then jumped at the noise. Through a window in the door, he spotted a small cat on the porch, staring up at him with accusing eyes. "Neptune," he said. Ollie smiled and let the sleek black cat in. Mystery solved. That's what he'd heard, his sweet Neptune.

Oliver sipped his tea, staring out into the starry night, knowing he needed sleep and strength for what the new day would bring. He hated confrontations, but he couldn't let this go. It was wrong. Against the law, he thought. He drained the last liquid from the cup and rested back against the counter, his thin bathrobe leaving his body unprotected from the cold marble edge. He'd go back upstairs, read that little collection of Loren Eisley's essays that Halley had given him. Fall asleep with visions of galaxies filling his head. And he'd deal with tomorrow, tomorrow.

Oliver left his mother's pink Limoges teacup in the sink and headed for the stairs. The tea had done its magic and a dreamy fog settled over him. He pulled himself up the first step, then another. Sleep. It was on its way.

Oliver reached the first landing where the steps curved back upon themselves and a small window lighted his path. He paused for a minute, taking in a breath of air, then frowned as the brightness of the stars beyond the window dimmed.

An eclipse? No, of course not. But things were moving in slow motion. The tree branches, leaves falling. Humming.

So odd, Ollie thought, and released his hold of the walnut railing. A dance. He was dancing, moving slowly through the air.

Neptune stood at the foot of the stairs, her green eyes watching as Oliver's long slender body turned slightly, then bent at the waist, doubled over, and slowly somersaulted down to the wide-planked kitchen floor.

Neptune meowed, then walked over to Oliver's face and gently licked his moist sharp chin with her gravely tongue.

CHAPTER 1

News of Ollie Harrington's death caused a ripple of deep sadness through the Canterbury University community and the neighborhood where his family had lived for generations. But a larger ripple—nearly a tidal wave, Po Paltrow thought—occurred when Ollie's twin sister, Adele, elegant and self-assured, swept down upon the small town of Crestwood a few days later to bury her brother.

Shades of Isadora Duncan, Po thought, the first day she spotted Adele speeding down Elderberry Road in her long elegant Cadillac convertible, a yellow scarf tied around her neck and flying in the autumn breeze. *She is certainly a whirlwind*. But the thought that Adele's arrival would cause the chaos that followed, was beyond Po's imagination.

Adele's years away had made her an unfamiliar figure to most residents, but in the space of a week she had quickly and efficiently buried her brother, taken over the Harrington mansion, disturbed quiet neighbors with strident demands to trim trees and keep children away from her property, and alienated nearly everyone else in town.

Even in the back room of Selma Parker's quilt shop on Elderberry Road, the Queen Bees quilting group, gathering for their Saturday morning session, felt the mounting tension.

"Like who would have imagined a quiet nice man like Oliver Harrington would have a sister like *that*!" said Phoebe Mellon, the youngest member of the group, as she looked around the cluttered table for a pair of scissors.

Eleanor Canterbury handed them to Phoebe. "It's a shame. Adele came to bury her brother. But she's doing damage to the Harrington name with her demands and rude manners." A rare note of displeasure crept into the lively voice of the Queen Bees' only octogenarian. Eleanor picked up a square of flowered red fabric and examined it carefully to see if she had left any stray threads hanging. Eleanor did all her piecing by hand—mostly because it was portable that way, she said, and she could take it with her to Paris or New Guinea or wherever she might be headed. Today she was finishing a table runner for a charity auction, and decided she had done a very nice job, indeed, on the crazy quilt design.

"But you can't say it isn't exciting, El," Phoebe replied.

"Even moms in my twins' playgroup are gabbing about her. Word has it she eats three-year olds." Phoebe dipped her blonde-white head and bit off a piece of thread.

Po Paltrow—Portia in more formal circles—laughed at Phoebe's irreverent comment, the kind they'd come to expect from her. She looked down to the end of the table at Selma Parker. "Selma, what do you think is up with Adele? I remember her from the neighborhood when we were growing up. And she was in your class, right?"

"A few years behind me," Selma said. She wet one finger, then touched the iron to be sure it was hot. The Saturday quilt group had met in the back of Parker's fabric store for as long as anyone could remember—beginning back when Selma's mother ran the shop. Members changed, of course, as life ran its course—daughters and granddaughters and sometimes friends of original members taking their place. And Selma loved it all—especially the present group of Queen Bees—an unlikely mixture of women with an age span of nearly sixty years, anchored on either end by Phoebe and Eleanor. Though the group had begun as quilting companions, their lives had become as intricately entwined as the strips of fabric they deftly fashioned into works of art.

Satisfied that the iron was hot and sewing machine was ready to go, Selma looked back at Po and nodded. "Adele didn't stick around Crestwood long, as you remember, Po. She came back for a short while after graduating from Smith College. But she couldn't settle down. I remembered her mother urging her to go back East. Encouraging her to leave. She told her that Crestwood wasn't big enough for her.

There seemed to be some tension in the family, but it was never talked about, of course. Walter Harrington was a pompous, arrogant, man—"

"Aha," Maggie Helmers interrupted, "it's in the genes, maybe."

"I remember Adele not liking it here," Po said, "And once she left, she rarely came back. I don't think she liked Crestwood very much."

"And apparently that hasn't changed," Kate Simpson said. She pushed her chair back from the table and took a sip of her coffee, careful not to spill it on the mounds of fat quarters piled on the table. "The neighborhood kids are already calling her the wicked witch of the north. But I feel kind of sorry for her. This can't be easy for her, coming back to bury her twin brother. Maybe this is how she handles grief. She's probably not so bad." Kate had come back to Crestwood to bury her own mother several years before—and the memory was still fresh, though cushioned now as sweet memories filled in around her loss.

"Bad? Kate, she's downright nasty," Maggie said. "She brought her dog into my clinic yesterday. The waiting room was packed because Daisy Sample's beagle was hit by a car. He's fine now. But anyway, Adele elbowed her way to the counter and demanded that Emerson be seen immediately. She was so rude. And then—" Maggie's hands gestured while she talked, and she waved several pieces of freezer paper onto the floor. "And then when Mandy—my new technician—tried to calm her down and explain why she'd have to wait, Adele told her she had bad breath and should see a dentist."

Po shook her head. She picked up a finished block of her quilt hanging and held it up to the light to check the hand stitching she'd done on the abstract design. She was trying something new—piecing together bright oranges and yellows and minty green strips in wavy swooshes. She'd hang it in the upper hallway, she thought, where it would brighten up the interior space. "I agree with Kate," she said. "Adele has had a rough couple weeks. Burying her brother and figuring out what to do with that enormous house and property can't be easy."

"People offered to help, Po," Leah Sarandon said. Leah, one of the most popular professors at Canterbury University, taught women's studies on the ivy-covered campus just a few blocks from the Harrington home in the oldest section of Crestwood. "Professor Fellers talked the college board into having a memorial service for Oliver. Jed Fellers was Ollie's mentor and spent a lot of time with him. Ollie was such a sweet guy—a little different—but he loved the library and learning and the college. And the students kind of adopted him because he was around all the time. Anyway, Adele said no. And there wasn't a funeral, either. As for selling the house, that won't be a problem at all. The college has tried to wrest it from Ollie for years. They may finally get it now."

"It's a magnificent estate," Po said. "I remember going to parties there when Adele and Oliver's parents were alive. And I stopped by now and then when I saw Ollie around, just to say hello, to take him some cobbler or bread. He'd always been a bit of a loner."

"The house is haunted," Phoebe said. "That's what Shelly Rampey in the kids' playgroup says. But that can be, like, good, depending on the ghosts, I guess. Shelly said that her yoga teacher is wanting to buy the place for a retreat house for busy mothers—a place they can go to refresh their spirits. I said, 'sign me up, sister.'"

"Phoebe, if your spirit were any more refreshed, we'd have to tie you down," Po said.

Phoebe laughed.

"But I agree with Leah," Po went on. "That property is priceless. Neighbors are concerned that it be sold to the right person."

"What's that mean?" Kate asked. She reached over to the table behind her for a pastry from Marla's bakery, just a few stores down on Elderberry Road.

"Well, the neighbors don't want anything that will bring traffic, that sort of thing. And there are so many beautiful old magnolias and oaks and pines on that property—the thought of a developer tearing it down and putting up huge new side-by-side houses is very sad. I think it's one of the oldest houses in Crestwood. It needs to be taken care of properly."

"Do you think Adele Harrington will care about any of that?" Eleanor asked.

"The house has been in the family for over 100 years," Po said. "Adele will surely consider that and do the right thing." But Po frowned as she spoke. The controversy surrounding the beautiful old home at 210 Kingfish Drive was heating up discussions in all pockets of life in sleepy Crestwood. And just this morning, as she ran past the Harrington home on her daily jog, she'd noticed that activity had picked up around the house—cars, and even a truck or two, driving in and out of the long, angular drive leading up to the stately home. Probably interested buyers coming to check it out, she had thought, though the hour was early and she wondered if the noise had awakened the neighbors. She'd noticed a truck with Tom Adler's Prairie Development name on it. He was hungry for more land to build homes on, Po knew. 210 Kingfish Drive would be wonderful for his needs.

"I'm not sure I share your confidence in Adele's sense of what's right, Po," Selma said. "She doesn't live here, after all, and doesn't give a hoot about the town." Selma sat with her back to the archway leading into the main room of the store, one ear on the customers being helped by two college girls who helped out on Saturdays. "There's so much money at stake. That's what will decide what happens to that beautiful home—money. Mark my words. And let's just hope it helps the town, not hurts it."

"Why Selma Parker," a new voice interjected itself into the mix. "Who would ever dream of hurting this little town?" Eight heads moved in unison and all eyes focused on the tall, commanding figure standing in the archway, directly behind Selma.

The woman smiled slightly, acknowledging them as a group. Then her gray eyes focused on Selma, and she took a step into the room. "Please, don't let me interrupt, ladies. Go on with your chitchat. I find your foolish conversation quite amusing."

Selma stood and wiped the palms of her sweaty hands down her rumpled tan slacks. Then she lifted one hand out in greeting and forced a smile to her face. "Hello, Adele," she said. "It's been a long time."

CHAPTER 2

Adele Harrington placed her Ballenciaga bag on the table.

"Yes, it has been a long time, Selma." Adele turned her long, angular face toward Po. "And Portia Paltrow," she said, her eyes moving slowly up and down Po, then settling in on her face. "You've aged agreeably, I see."

Po felt the tension in the room but forced a smile to her face. "We were all terribly sad to hear about Oliver, Adele." Adele waved her long fingers through the air as if dismissing Po's thought. "Death happens," she said. "Perhaps Oliver would have lived longer if he hadn't shut himself up in that

house like a damn monk. He was a genius, you know."
Adele surveyed the group. She looked at Phoebe for a long
time and then shook her head. "Did you cut your hair with
a lawn clippers?" she asked finally.

Shortly after Jude and Emma were born, Phoebe had
clipped her gold mane short all over her head. And she
loved the freedom of the no-nonsense, one-inch style.
Eleanor called her the Queen Bees' platinum-haired pixie.
It was a look that could look beautiful only on Phoebe
Mellon.

Phoebe smiled sweetly at Adele and cocked her head
to one side. "A FlowBee and scissors. Easy as pie. Want
me to do yours?"

Adele's hand shot up instinctively to her thick shoulder-
length hair. It lacked the sprinkling of gray that most wom-
en in their fifties coped with, and this morning it floated
loosely about her attractive face. "You're married to that
Mellon boy," she said.

"Is there something you wanted, Adele?" Selma asked,
dismissing the moment and hoping Phoebe wouldn't run
for her FlowBee. Phoebe didn't allow herself to be pushed
around readily. "Would you like a cup of coffee?"

Adele was silent a moment, as if considering the question, then looked over at Phoebe again. "I like her spunk,"
she said to no one in particular. "Yes, Selma. Please bring
me a cup of coffee."

Po wondered if Adele had spent the years away from
Crestwood managing a flock of servants. Nevertheless,
Po, being closest to the side table holding the coffeepot

and the usual stash of flaky pastries from Marla's bakery, poured a cup for Adele. "Cream and sugar are on the table," she said, handing the cup to Adele and nodding toward the sideboard.

"Black is fine," Adele said and turned back to Selma. "Though you haven't offered the usual amenity, Selma, I would like to sit down. May I? I want to talk with all of you."

A questioning look passed between Selma and Po as they wondered in tandem what in the world Adele Harrington wanted with them.

Selma touched the iron to see if it was hot and then looked back at Adele. "This is the Queen Bees quilting group, Adele, and they meet here in my shop every Saturday morning. Certainly you may sit, but we'll want to continue finishing up our—"

"I know what this is, Selma," Adele cut in. "My mother was a Queen Bee, lest you forget."

From her corner chair, Eleanor smiled, remembering. "Of course she was. She was an excellent quilter and a very lovely woman." *And how in the world did she bear the likes of you*, Eleanor thought.

Adele looked over at Eleanor, noticing the elegant gray-haired woman for the first time. "Eleanor Canterbury?" she said. "My God, are you still alive?"

Eleanor's delicious laughter floated above the cluttered table. "I suppose that's a matter of opinion, Adele. But yes, I believe I am. Would you like a pinch?" She held out her arm. Dangly gold bracelets chimed against one another.

Adele stared at Eleanor for a moment. "Amazing," she said, shaking her head. "My mother liked you, if I remember correctly."

"Your mother liked everyone, Adele," Eleanor said.

"You're wrong about that, Eleanor." Adele smiled politely, pulled out a chair and sat down. "You may continue with your work, but I would like to tell you why I am here."

"That would be nice," Selma said, and she picked up an all-white, whole-cloth quilt hanging that she had made for a new stationery store opening up down the road. In the center of the piece, Selma had designed a delicate feather pen and scrolled piece of paper, intricately stitching the design and framing it with a cable pattern. The background was filled in with a grid pattern—millions of tiny stitches that resulted in a beautifully designed work of art.

"How cool, Selma!" Phoebe leaned over the shopowner's shoulder and touched the stitching with the tip of her finger. "That's perfect for the stationery store!" Though the Bees sometimes worked on a single project together, for the past few months they had worked on individual projects, guided by Leah and Susan, who were always there to help with design and color and fabric.

Adele cleared her throat, pulling the attention back to her.

"Adele, do you know the others?" Po asked.

Adele glanced around the table. "I know who most of you are. I've checked the group out, of course."

Po frowned. Checked them out? What on earth was Adele Harrington thinking, coming in and confronting them this way?

"You're Kate Simpson," Adele said, looking at Kate. Her tone was accusatory.

Even in jeans and a t-shirt, her normal Saturday attire, Kate stood out in a crowd. She was the tallest Bee by several inches, as slender as Kansas wheat, and had thick, unruly auburn hair and arresting brown eyes that could stop traffic, even in sleepy Crestwood. And Kate backed down to few people.

She looked evenly at Adele. "I am," she said simply. She decided not to remind Adele that they had met several times, and that she lived just a couple blocks from the Harrington mansion. It probably wouldn't matter to her, Kate decided.

"I've seen you riding that fool bike past the house," Adele said. Then, abruptly, she looked at Maggie and nodded, recognition softening the sculpted lines of her face. "I've met you, Dr. Helmers," she said. "You were good to my Emerson."

Maggie nodded. "Emerson is a wonderful dog."

Adele nodded, and it was clear that Emerson held a special spot in her life. Maggie decided that though she didn't much care for the woman, her affection for Emerson won her a couple of points. Maybe.

Leah Sarandon had been watching Adele carefully, wondering if she would recognize her. A few years before Leah had been on a committee that granted an award for writing to a college student. That year Ollie Harrington, an older student who had returned to college after years away, was the winner, chosen for an essay he'd written on the Milky Way. It was sparse and elegant, and did indeed appear to be the work of a genius, as Adele had stated earlier. Jed Fellers, an astronomy professor at Canterbury, had taken Ollie under his wing and nurtured the talent that was most deserving of the award. Adele Harrington had come to town, a rare occasion, to attend the banquet honoring her brother. Leah remembered her being rather aloof but seemingly proud of her brother.

"And you are?" Adele asked now. "You don't appear to be a Crestwood native."

She didn't remember, Leah thought, which was fine. "I'm from the East Coast, Adele, but my husband and I have lived here for awhile. I teach at Canterbury and my husband is a pediatrician here in town."

"And you do some of the design work with this group?"

"Some. I like to try new things with the group. They indulge me."

"Good. And in answer to your unasked question—yes, I remember you from the banquet honoring my brother. I never forget a face, though your name escaped me."

Adele's piercing eyes studied Leah for a moment, then moved on to Susan Miller, Selma's shop assistant. Susan, like Ollie Harrington, had returned to get a college degree later than most. In Susan's case, it was Selma who convinced her helper that thirty-five was the perfect age, and someone with Susan's talent for fiber design shouldn't be hiding it in a small sewing store with a chubby proprietress. And so Susan had registered at Canterbury University, and her knowledge of fabric and shapes and colors was a gift the Queen Bees counted on in creating the most beautiful quilts in Kansas. "You put together that quilt display in the library," Adele said finally.

"Leah and I put that together," Susan said. The reading room in the college library often displayed the artwork of students, faculty, and sometimes residents. Recently they'd featured a variety of quilts honoring life on the Kansas prairie, all designed and quilted by Kansas women.

"It's a lovely display," Adele said. The sudden compliment caused Po to laugh lightly. Adele Harrington was a package of contradictions. "Adele Harrington, I believe you are all show," she said. "Now, why are you here and what do you want? We're always happy to have visitors, but we're busy, as you can see. And I am sure you are busy, too, getting that huge house ready for an eager market."

"An eager market?"

"I'd say that everyone from the college board of directors to the city council to outside investors would like nothing better than to be the proud owners of your beautiful ten acres and that amazing house." Po took a sip of coffee.

"Is that what this silly town thinks?"

Po frowned, not understanding Adele's comment, but not inclined to ask for an explanation. Instead, she continued in her own direction. "Those of us in the neighborhood are hoping you'll be discriminating when you decide who will own it next. Large condos wouldn't endear you to the neighbors." Po chose her words carefully. She had no right to tell Adele what to do with her inheritance, but she hoped that she cherished her family's house enough to be careful about what happened to it. And Po herself wasn't sure what that would be. The days of single families living in mansions were pretty much over, and although she'd love for the house to be preserved, she wasn't sure what the best choice would be. Perhaps a small museum to house local art? Something that wouldn't cause traffic jams, something tasteful and discrete.

"And do you think I care about being liked by the neighbors, Po?" Adele asked.

"Yes," Po said simply. And in that moment, Po believed her own words. There was something forced about Adele's attitude. Po remembered Adele as a young woman, home from her first year at Smith. She had come over one day with her mother, shortly after newlyweds Po and Sam had moved into the home she still lived in. Po remembered with some clarity because Adele was excited about the things she was learning and the thrill of living near Boston and soaking up all it had to offer. Po wasn't that far removed from her own experience at Radcliffe, and they had shared stories about football games and clubs and what once were the Seven Sister schools.

Adele had seemed older than her years even then, but her enthusiasm for life and learning had impressed Po. The austere façade she had adopted in her early fifties didn't seem a totally comfortable fit, and Po wondered if this was the real Adele they were seeing or if grief and loss had hardened her.

"Po's right, Adele," Selma said. "Everyone is welcome here, but we've projects to finish. Is there something in particular we can help you with?"

"Of course there is. I don't make a habit of wasting my

Saturday mornings in the backrooms of small shops." She paused and looked around the table, taking in each of the women and the fabric in front of them. Nearly finished table runners and small colorful quilts ready to hang on walls crowded the table.

The Queen Bees were all watching Adele, their fingers the only movement in the room.

Adele placed the palms of her hands on the table as if addressing a jury. "I'm here on business. I want you to make eight quilts for me."

Eight sets of fingers ceased movement, as if hit by a bolt of lightning.

"Immediately," Adele added.

"What?" Selma said.

"You heard me, Selma Parker. I want you to make eight quilts for me," Adele repeated. "I will pay you plenty— you can donate it to that quilt museum I hear you want to start, or whatever." Her long thin fingers waved the air. "I will even donate extra to the cause. I want fine pieced quilt tops—I have already made arrangements to have them quilted as soon as you are finished piecing them. And I want you to begin working on them now."

"Why in heaven's name do you want eight quilts?"

"I want twelve quilts. But my mother preserved some of her own, and I will use four of those."

"For what?" Kate asked.

"For the bed and breakfast I will be opening in my family home."

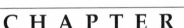

C H A P T E R 3

The news that Adele Harrington was turning the Harrington mansion into a B&B hit Crestwood with the force of a Kansas tornado.

The issue wasn't that the bed and breakfast idea was foreign to residents — Crestwood was the perfect atmosphere for a cozy B&B, and the town already boasted two small inns near the Emerald River. Parents of Canterbury students kept them full and profitable. It was that the Harrington property was probably the most valuable private home in the entire town—and folks had an eye on it for far more lofty enterprises than a place for visitors to spend the night and wake up to omelets and home-made cinnamon rolls.

A special meeting was called to protest the conversion of the mansion into a business, and Po felt the venom in her neighbor's speech.

"There'll be traffic messes, ungodly noise—and they'll probably start having weddings and God knows what over there," Keith Harris had bellowed. But listening quietly in the corner of the Harris's living room, Po knew it was more than that. It was the change in the quiet, tree-canopied neighborhoods that they all feared. A B&B this year, and what would be next? It was the fact that a park on that land would solidify the area near the college as a coveted place to live. It was the loss of control over what happened to their neighborhood and perhaps a dip in property values. And of course, it was money. If Adele held onto the property, others couldn't make a tidy fortune of their own.

But Adele had bested them all, finding loopholes in the zoning law for a home that had graced the land before most of Crestwood even existed. It was going to be a bed and breakfast. And there was nothing anyone in all of Crestwood could do about it.

"People are so mad that I'm almost ashamed we're helping her," Kate said to Po as they wandered about the city market late Saturday morning. Kate swallowed a bite of apple. "On the other hand, it's a fun project."

Today's quilt session had been an enthusiastic one, with ideas for the Harrington quilts bouncing off the walls. In the end, they'd decided to focus on traditional patterns for most of the B&B's rooms, using old patterns stored away from the *Kansas City Star* newspaper collection. The familiar patterns would be perfect for a bed and breakfast, they'd all agreed. Picking eight from the thousand that had been published would be the hard part.

"It will be a challenge, Kate. But I agree—lots of fun." Po stopped at an apple booth and felt the Jonathan apples. They'd be perfect for a pie, she thought.

Though summer squash had given way to pumpkins and homegrown apples, the market was still buzzing with activities. Situated on the banks of the Emerald River, the open-air market was part of a cleaned-up area that had given rise in recent years to a park and restaurants dotting the downtown area. Run by farmers and residents from around the area who brought in organic produce and herbs and flowers from May to late September, the market was a vibrant place for visitors and townsfolk to gather on sunny Saturday mornings. The smell of fritters and hot coffee filled the air, and on most Saturdays a local group of musicians played in the small white gazebo while children danced on its steps and old folks filled the benches and clapped their hands or nodded to the music.

Po picked up a jar of pesto sauce and read the hand-lettered label. "You're right about this B&B causing a fuss," she said, and told Kate about the neighborhood meeting. "It isn't making Adele any friends, not that she seems to want them."

Murder on a Starry Night

It had been one week since Adele had dropped her bombshell to the Bees, and for seven days the *Crestwood Daily News* had been full of letters to the editor protesting the decision.

"You don't have to tell me what you're talking about." Leah walked over to her two friends from a nearby pumpkin stand. "Who would have thought one woman could have created such a stir?" Leah's denim skirt swept her ankles and a chunky necklace moved on her hand-screened tee shirt as she talked. Leah's distinctive look of dress and jewelry was often imitated by students who fought tooth and nail to get into her classes.

"Frankly, Leah, I've decided a lot worse things could go in there than a B&B," Po said. "There will be twelve bedrooms, that's maybe 25 people at one time plus staff. Not exactly a traffic jam."

"Maybe it's the idea that she's going to be living here that's infuriating people," Kate said. "She isn't exactly a warm and welcoming inn keeper-type."

"There's some truth in that," said Po. "But I think it's the disappointed parties that are causing the furor. People who wanted the property for their own interests."

"I can vouch for the college's fury," Leah said. "Canterbury U. was Ollie's second home. He was there daily, even after he finally had a degree in his pocket. I think he came alive under Jed Feller's tutelage. He was always so patient and encouraging of Ollie and let him sit in on his astronomy classes whenever he wanted. The kids teased Ollie sometimes—but they learned to like him, too. But anyway, Ollie had actually told

Chancellor Phillips that he'd will the house to Canterbury when he died."

"It appears he didn't get around to doing that," Po said. "Max Elliot has handled the Harrington affairs forever, and he said Ollie never put anything in writing. Ollie cared more about things like black holes and planets' orbits than he did about wills."

"It's too bad. Canterbury would have maintained the house's integrity," Leah said. She waved at a group of college students walking by.

Po nodded. "They'd have been a better choice than Tom Adler and his Prairie Development group—I hear Oliver also told them that they could have the house. They actually had a plan in place that they'd shown Oliver. Tom promised he'd keep the lovely grounds as best he could, but the plan was five homes on the land—luxury homes for empty nesters, they described it. I suppose that means people like me."

Kate laughed. She picked up a bunch of slender asparagus and a clump of arugula and handed some bills to the young girl behind the stand. "Po, you may think your nest is empty with the kids living on the West Coast, but it will never be true. Has there ever been even a week without a gathering at the Paltrow home? I doubt it." Po's home had been a second home to Kate nearly all her life, and especially since her mother's death a couple of years earlier.

"I guess you're right. It doesn't feel empty, that I know for sure. And maybe that's Adele's dream—to fill the Harrington house with people. It's been a shell for a long time. Oliver always liked it when I stopped by, and I know he had a few friends, but he wasn't much of a party giver."

"Have you been inside the home recently, Po?"

"A few times. Ollie and I mostly sat on the veranda and talked. He'd go on for hours about stars and galaxies—I think he had read every book ever written on planet alignments. He was such a sweet man. I'd see him every day walking over to campus. As you said, Leah, that was his life."

"Oliver would probably have liked the college having his house."

"Yes," Po agreed. "But it's not to be. So we need to move on."

"I talked to Susan after our session today about the quilts," Leah said. "By next Saturday, we should have materials picked out and ready to go. I'm going to meet Adele at the house today to look at colors. Want to come?"

"Sure," Kate said immediately. "Wow, a preview. Po, you come, too."

"I need to run by the college library briefly, but that's all that's on my schedule until the reception tonight at Canterbury," Po said. "I'll be happy to go."

"Oh, dear, I nearly forgot about the party," Leah said. "Eleanor is such a sport to host it. I don't know what the college would do without her."

"I think the whole town must be invited," Kate said. "Even P.J. got invited."

"Even P.J.?" Po teased. Kate's current relationship with P.J. Flanigan, a member of the Crestwood police department and one-time lawyer, pleased Po to no end. She'd known

P.J. nearly as long as she'd known Kate; a kinder, more trustworthy man couldn't be found. And his sense of humor and laid-back personality helped, too. One definitely needed that to be involved with Kate. "Of course P.J. would be invited," Po said. "Eleanor figures her payback for hosting university affairs at her home is the license to invite all her friends."

"To make it fun, she told me," Kate said.

Po laughed, "That's true. Those events can be mighty dull on occasion. I can't even remember what this one is for. But I know Eleanor was in the mood for a party and she probably jumped at the chance to have it at her house."

"It's for several faculty members who have had things published recently. Jed Fellers is one of them," Leah said. "I'm going just for him. He's such a nice guy, and he's been trying for eons to get something published. There's so much pressure on faculty now that Canterbury is a university that we're all overjoyed when someone makes it to print."

"Well, good for Professor Fellers. I took his introduction to astronomy class a couple years ago and it was great," Kate said. "He's a terrific teacher."

"It's nice the college gives credit where it's due," Po said. "My Sam would approve—and he'd be happy about Jed. He's been at the college a long time, so this is a good thing for him."

"You're right, Po. Sam would like this—both the recognition for the faculty and the excuse for a party," Kate said, speaking fondly of her godfather.

Po agreed. "Sam loved a good excuse for a party."

"And no matter what the party's for, it'll get our minds off Adele Harrington for a while," Kate said.

"Who seems to show up everywhere," Leah nodded toward a family-run booth across the crowded aisle. Loaves of fresh homemade povitica from Kansas City's Strawberry Hill filled the table. Adele Harrington was leaning in toward the young woman behind the table. The salesperson fidgeted, moving from one foot to another and casting sideways looks at her mother as if pleading for help. Finally Adele shook her finger in the girl's face, set the loaf of povitica back down and abruptly turned and walked away. The young woman looked after her with tears in her eyes.

"Another fallen bird in Adele's path," Po murmured. "What is it with this lady?"

Po wove her way across the aisle and picked up the loaf of cream-cheese bread. Adele's fingerprints were visible on the wrapping where she had pinched the rich coffee cake. She smiled at the young girl. "This looks delicious. I'd like this loaf please."

"I'll get you a fresh one. The lady squeezed this one, I'm afraid."

"That's all right. It will taste just as good, don't you think?"

The young girl smiled gratefully at Po and fumbled in the large pocket of her apron for change. "She is going to buy our poviticas for her inn," she said. "But I think we will earn every penny of it."

"Yes, my dear," Po replied. "I suspect you will."

Adele Harrington, from two stalls up, turned suddenly

and looked over the heads of several young mothers pushing strollers. "Po Paltrow," she called out over the market din.

"I expect you should come today, too. And you shouldn't buy damaged goods. It's not responsible."

Adele turned and walked on down the row of stands, her head held high and her eyes looking out toward the river, as if planning her next step. Po watched her disappear along the river walk, wondering with some sadness what was going on inside Adele Harrington. And a sixth sense that her mother often warned her about, told her she might be better off not knowing. Sometimes, there's safety in ignorance.

Po gathered up her cloth sacks, heavy now with fall's bountiful produce and hurried after Kate and Leah.

CHAPTER 4

The Harrington mansion was noisy with activity when Po met Susan and Kate at the end of the driveway an hour later. The long drive that lead up to the three-story stone house was lined with trucks, and men in overalls and jeans carried pails and heavy tool boxes back and forth.

"Adele doesn't waste any time," Kate said, dodging a ladder swinging from a short, no-nonsense man's shoulder.

"The place is certainly getting a top-notch manicure," Po said.

"It's pure Gatsby," Kate mused. "All I need is a martini."

Tall pines lined the perimeters and enormous oak trees shaded the yard, their gnarled branches angling out in all directions. The tips of maple trees were beginning to turn red, heralding the heart of fall. And everywhere, there were freshly tilled patches of earth where brilliant mums bloomed.

"You don't get a sense of this place from the road," Leah said. "It's magnificent. I can't believe Ollie lived here all alone."

"I wonder if he was lonely," Po said. "He didn't seem to be, but one wonders." Po watched several men working in a shade garden along the side of the property beneath a canopy of trees. Where once volunteer trees and bushes crowded the wrought iron fence, now smooth, rich soil welcomed hostas and red twig dogwoods and hydrangeas.

Po wondered briefly what had happened to Joe Bates, the long-time gardener who had been on staff at the Harrington home as long as she could remember—a nice old man who had an amazing way with flowers. As un-kempt as the property sometimes was in recent years when Joe couldn't get around to everything, the small plots he tended around the back pond were always perfect. He was always somewhere around when she visited Ollie, puttering in his flowerbeds, eyeing anyone who came near the house like a watchdog. And she wondered now if Adele had kept him on, or if he had become a casualty of the land-scapers turning the lawns and gardens into works of art.

"Looking for Miz Harrington?" a young painter asked as they approached the wide front porch. He was perched on a ladder, a paint can swinging precariously from a hook at the top.

"Yes," Leah answered. "Is she around?"

The man took his baseball hat off and wiped his brow, then pointed to the side of the house. "She's out back. Not in the best of moods today, just a warning to y'all. Follow the roar and you'll find her easy enough." He grinned, then tugged his cap back on and returned to painting the top edge of the porch.

Po, Kate, and Leah followed his directive and walked along the stone path that circled the house. Windows were flung wide open to catch the cool breezes of early fall, and inside were sounds of more activity—furniture being moved, sanders grinding away years of footprints from the hardwood floors.

"There she is," Leah said, pointing to a gazebo situated in a grove of trees.

"I think there's someone with her," Po said, squinting in the bright sunlight as they walked along the slate pathway toward the gazebo.

As they got closer, their steps were stilled by Adele's voice, loud and clear—and definitely not happy.

"Foolish, brazen young woman!" Adele hissed. "How dare you come to my home uninvited. Leave immediately, or I shall have you arrested."

"You're destroying Oliver's birthright," a softer voice answered. "He never, ever intended his home to become a commercial property."

"I've stolen nothing, and you are entirely out of line, young lady."

"Ollie was a decent, good man. And...and he didn't die from a fall down the stairs. You know that and so do I!"

Adele lifted her hand abruptly, then just as quickly let it fall to her side, She spun away from the woman, staring into the faces of the three visitors. For a brief moment, she appeared disoriented, then just as quickly, a polished smile spread across her face.

"Hello, ladies," she said evenly, glancing at a thin gold watch on her wrist. "You're on time. That's good." She walked down the three gazebo steps toward them, leaving her visitor standing awkwardly behind her.

The woman stared after Adele. Her green eyes shot angry darts toward the older woman's back. For a brief moment, Po was afraid she was going to fling her backpack at the back of Adele's head. Instead, the pony-tailed woman brushed past Adele and hurried down the steps. She nodded politely at the three women. Then stopped short, a blush of embarrassment coloring her cheeks as she met Leah's smile of recognition. She started to speak, then thought better of it and hurried along the path leading around the side of the house.

Po watched her walk away. She was pleasant-looking in a casual, earthy way, with a sprinkling of freckles across a straight nose. Po guessed her age at thirty-five or so. She looked vaguely familiar, but then, she had the kind of shy face you could have passed dozens of times in Dillons or Marla's bakery without really noticing. A nice face, nevertheless.

The woman saw Joe Bates as he walked down the back stairs of the garage apartment. She paused on the path to wave at the gardener. Joe squinted, then smiled in recognition and called out a hello. Then he spotted Adele, and immediately turned and began the long trek back up the stairs.

"We didn't mean to interrupt," Leah was saying to Adele.

"You didn't interrupt. We have an appointment, do we not?" Adele looked at Leah and lifted one brow. She made no reference to the unpleasant encounter they had just witnessed, and instead, waved them toward the house. "I want you to see the bedrooms, though they're in a state of disrepair right now. But the colors are important, and I suspect you will be able to feel the warmth and ambience and plan your quilts accordingly."

As the women toured the magnificent second and third stories of the house—where guests would soon be catered to in the finest way—they were awed by the beauty of the old home. It had twelve bedrooms in all, Adele explained, and each would have its own bath. Some rooms boasted small sitting rooms off the bedroom and had balconies that looked out over the long expanse of backyard and gardens and the small pond. Although some rooms were now stripped of furniture and rugs, others, which Po suspected had been the family's quarters, still had books on the shelves and personal items cluttering tall secretaries and dressers and walnut armoires.

A closet door, slightly ajar, showed dresses and silk robes hanging on hangers as if waiting for someone to wear them. She imagined it must look exactly like it did when Adele was a girl living at 210 Kingfish Drive.

As they wandered in and out of the rooms, Po wondered which one had been Oliver's. It was on the backside of the house, she knew, because he often told her about standing at his window at night and seeing the stars reflected in the pond.

"Oliver never wanted me to touch a thing after our parents died," Adele said, as if reading Po's thought. "As a result, the house is jammed packed with things. He never discarded anything. Every drawer is full. I am weeding away at it, little by little, but it will take years." She moved down the hallway and ushered the women into a room at the very end. The room was smaller than the others, and simply adorned with a single bed between two large windows, a dresser, several bookcases, and a desk. A large telescope was positioned in front of one of the windows, pointing toward the sky.

Po walked over and looked at the books on the shelves, mostly astronomy texts and readings about nature, all arranged alphabetically and their spines lined up perfectly on the shelf. "This must have been Oliver's room," she said aloud.

"Yes. It was the only room in the house that he would sleep in from the time he got his own bed. Oliver was as bright as they come, but a few learning disabilities made some things hard for him. But you probably know that. I know you all knew Ollie somewhat," Adele said. Her voice fell off then, and she looked around the room, memories weighing visibly on her shoulders. She picked up a book from the nightstand beside Ollie's bed. "Loren Eiseley's *Immense Journey*," she read.

"Ollie saw himself as a kind of Loren Eiseley, I think," Po said. "Part philosopher, part scientist. He had such a lovely way of describing the most learned astrological things." She looked at his desk, everything neat and orderly, a cup holding pencils on the side, a yellow pad of paper, and in the center of the desk, a book Po recognized: *A Plain Man's Guide to a Starry Night*. She picked it up and leafed through it. Clearly Ollie had read it—the book was filled with underlined sentences and notes in the margins.

Adele looked around the room, taking in the neatly made bed, the bookcases, the straight-backed chair. She looked at Po with an unexpected softness in her eyes. "Whatever the design of the quilt you make for this room, it must have stars on it," she said softly, then straightened her shoulders and walked briskly out of the room, followed by Kate and Leah, and on down the hall.

Po stood just outside the room for a minute, glancing at the landing of a narrow set of steps just outside Ollie's door. *Were these the steps that led to the kitchen?* she wondered. *The steps that led to Oliver's death?*

"Portia, are you coming?" Adele stood in the middle of the hallway, looking back at Po.

Po looked away from the stairs and smiled at Adele. "I was thinking about Oliver," she said simply.

"And what were you thinking about him?"

"I was thinking that falling down the stairs was a tragic way for him to die."

"But maybe fitting. An accident. Oliver's life, in a way, was an accident."

Po was startled by the unexpected anguish in Adele's voice. "Adele, Ollie was a good man. He didn't see his life that way," Po said.

"No, not at all," Leah said. "Ollie had a purpose to his life, especially these past years. He spent time writing, and he had interesting conversations with students and faculty. He had a good life, Adele."

Adele focused her attention on a Thomas Hart Benton painting hanging on the wall. Finally she pulled her eyes away from it and looked at the three women standing behind her. "I hope so," was all she said, and then, as if she hadn't spoken at all, ushered them down the main staircase, through a hallway, and out onto the stone patio that wrapped across the side and back of the house. "Breakfast will be served out here in nice weather," she said brightly. "Would you like to have a cup of tea?"

Po glanced at her watch. "We've stayed longer than we intended."

"Eleanor's party," Kate yelped.

"I've kept you from something?" Adele asked, her brow lifting.

"No," Po assured her. "It's not until this evening. But knowing Kate, she probably needs to find something to wear."

"To wear to what?" Adele asked.

Po was uncomfortable talking about a social event to someone who wasn't invited to it. And though Eleanor was always generous in her invitations, she doubted that she would have thought to invite Adele. Nor would she have been on the college list. "The college is having a small reception tonight at Eleanor Canterbury's home. It's done periodically to recognize faculty in one way or another."

"Who is being recognized?"

"Tonight it's faculty who have recently had something published," Leah said. "Publishing is very important to Canterbury, now that the college is a university."

"Publish or perish," Adele said.

"Kind of," Leah said. "And two or three of the faculty are being recognized tonight. It's a subtle push for others to follow, I think."

"The reception is something done periodically. It's nothing, really," Po said.

Adele listened to Po intently, a frown creasing her forehead. Then she shifted her attention, looking beyond the women, seemingly moving on to other things. She waved her hand in dismissal. "Please keep in touch with me about the quilts and your progress," she said. "I will need you to check with me periodically, and—"

A noise down the driveway drew their attention to the garage. Joe Bates, his body hunched over, was pushing an old wheelbarrow filled with dirt across the walkway. Clumps of mud fell onto the brick pathway as he moved.

Adele's fists dug into her hips and her voice grew hard. "He is an eyesore," she said. And then, without another glance at her guests, she walked quickly down the driveway after Joe.

For a brief moment, Po felt the need to beat her to her prey and to scoop old Joe Bates up and out of the way of Adele's seemingly ungrounded anger. Instead she watched as Adele approached the man, her hands flying through the air and her words burying him in a deluge of complaints.

"Let's get out of here," Kate said, heading down the driveway to their cars. "We might be Adele's next target."

CHAPTER 5

Po dropped Kate and Leah off and checked her watch. Nice timing. She could still get over to the library and look for that new book on the history of women in Kansas quilting circles. In recent years, Po's writing career had grown from articles in magazines and essays in literary journals—most often on the history of women and the arts—to a short book here or there. And both Gus Schuette's bookstore on Elderberry Road and Canterbury library were indispensable to her.

Po pulled into the faculty lot and parked her car—a luxury

Murder on a Starry Night

that being married to a past president afforded her—and climbed the wide fan of steps leading up to the front door. As she went to pull open the heavy glass door, Jed Fellers smiled out at her from the other side. He pushed open the door with one hand and held it for Po.

"Thanks, Jed," Po said. Jedson Fellers had come to Canterbury late in Sam Paltrow's tenure as president. She and Sam had both liked the man with the easy smile and had attended many of his eloquent lectures on everything from black holes to exploring the cosmic dark ages.

"What brings you to our halls of learning, Po?" Jed asked, shifting his arms to accommodate a heavy stack of books.

"I'm here to pick up a few books, Jed, just like yourself. I hear you have a book out. Is this for number two?" She nodded at the pile of books in his arms.

Jed laughed. "Maybe down the road. Definitely not now. I'm just trying to keep one step ahead of my students."

"Leah says that Ollie Harrington was a friend of yours."

Jed nodded. "Ollie was many things to me—an assistant, a student, mostly a friend, I guess," Jed answered. "He was... he was a breath of fresh air in my classroom. Kids get tired of the same voice, the same manner. But Ollie brought a charisma to a class. He was so honest, and so fresh in his approach to the heavens." Jed looked out over the green lawns, now colored with small piles of falling leaves. He forced a smile back to his face and focused again on Po. "I'll miss him."

Po watched the sadness play across Jed's strong features and thought about how many people Ollie had touched—

and probably never even knew it. He was the twin less noticed, the second born, the one who had to work harder to make his place in life, and what a fine job he had done. Po touched Jed's arm lightly. "That always plays two ways, Jed. You nurtured Ollie, gave him a sense of purpose. Helped make his time here satisfying."

Jed didn't answer, but he leaned over and lightly kissed her cheek. "Thanks, Po," he said softly, and slowly made his way down the steps.

Po turned and walked on into the main room. The library was busy for a Saturday, she thought, and then remembered that midterms were probably around the corner. Some of the reason for Jed's burden of books, she realized. She walked quickly over to the reserve desk where Leah had promised her she'd leave the book Po was looking for.

A pleasant looking woman, dressed in slacks and a tee shirt, her brown hair pulled back and held in place with a bright blue elastic band, looked up and smiled as Po approached.

Immediately her smile faded, and she looked down at the desk, embarrassed.

"Hello again," Po said. "I'm Po Paltrow."

The woman nodded. "I've seen you in here—and saw you today with Professor Sarandon. I'm Halley Peterson." Halley managed a small smile.

Po shook the woman's hand. "That was unpleasant for you. I'm sorry."

Halley pushed her glasses up into her hair. "I apologize for my behavior. Today hasn't been one of my best days."

"You were upset. There's no need to apologize."

"Ollie Harrington was a good friend of mine. He spent a lot of time here in the library. Did you know him?"

"Yes. We were neighbors. Ollie was a good man."

Halley nodded. "And he would have loved a decent burial with his friends around him. But Adele Harrington—" Halley broke off mid-sentence. "I'm sorry, I barely know you. You may be a friend of hers and I'm totally out of line speaking like this, Mrs. Paltrow."

"Please, Halley, call me Po. And I understand. Adele elicits strong responses in people," Po said. "It's clear you cared about her brother."

Halley's face seemed to be crumbling under Po's concerned look. Slender fingers groped for a water bottle sitting on the counter beside a pad of paper.

"Maybe you should sit down, Halley," Po said. She touched the woman's arm.

Halley shook her head. "I'm fine," she whispered. "But thank you." Halley leaned forward, her waist pressing into the high counter, her level gaze holding Po's attention. Her voice was low, but filled with an intensity that for a moment startled Po and seemed out of place in the mild-mannered woman.

"Someone needs to listen, Po," Halley Peterson said. Her hands were shaking now, making small thumping noises on the library desk, her green eyes lit with fire. "I don't think Ollie's death was normal. It wasn't right. I think...I think someone wanted Ollie Harrington to die."

CHAPTER 6

Po had had no time to respond. A student needing Halley's attention had cut short her conversation with the librarian, and she had checked out her books and left the library. Halley's outburst was curious, and Po wondered what she had meant. Surely she didn't mean those words literally. She was overwrought. A good friend had died. And she hadn't had a chance to say good-bye. But she would have to talk with Halley about it later—there wasn't time to process it now. Right now she needed get home and be ready when Max Elliot picked her up for Eleanor's cocktail party.

Po raced home, and in short order, she had showered

and slipped into a pair of silky black slacks and a bright blue wrap-around blouse that opened wide at the neck. Daily runs, though slower than a decade ago, kept Po's body limber and lean—and a glance in the full-length closet mirror confirmed that her slacks fit nicely, despite too many dinners at Picasso's French Quarter.

"Po, you up there?" Max Elliot stood at the foot of the staircase winding up to the second floor of Po's airy home, his hand on the walnut post. "And what did I tell you about locking these doors?"

"Ready in a minute, Max," Po called back, ignoring the gentle scolding, even though there was a reason for Max's admonition. A year before she and Max had both been in danger when a young man had let himself into her home through the open front door. Though thwarted in his efforts, his intent had been to harm. But Po still couldn't shake her belief that Crestwood was essentially a safe place to live, and unlocked doors had been the way she was raised.

Po stood in front of her dresser mirror and ran a brush through her salt and pepper hair. She'd thought about coloring it recently, but the extra time pulled from her busy days seemed not worth the while. Besides, Sam had always said he liked the white streaks highlighting her sable-colored hair.

"Nature's highlights," he'd called them.

Po quickly applied pale pink blush to her prominent cheekbones and applied a wisp of taupe shadow on her lids. A touch of lipstick and she was nearly set to go. Grabbing a black shawl from the back of a chair, she walked down the steps. "If I had locked the door, dear Max," she said, a note of playfulness in her voice, "how could you possibly have gotten in?"

Max smiled and kissed Po on the cheek, the familiar answer lost in the pleasure of seeing her. "I would have broken it down to see you. You look lovely, Po."

"Thank you, Max," Po said, pleased with the compliment. She slipped her arm through his and nodded toward the door. "Ready to party, my friend?"

Max held the door for her, then followed her down the walkway to his small silver Honda. Max was Crestwood's best-known lawyer and financial planner, having lived in the small Kansas town his whole life, with time away for college and law school at the University of Kansas, just a short drive from Crestwood. His parents and their parents before had lived in Crestwood, and Max not only knew nearly everyone in town, he knew their family secrets as well. A friend of Po and Sam Paltrow's for as long as Po could remember, Max became a trusted confidant when Sam died, helping Po sort through the investments and trusts Sam had left, assuring Po of a comfortable life. In recent months the two had slipped into the habit of attending movies and lectures and social gatherings together, and Po admitted to Leah last Sunday at breakfast that the nice-looking widower with the quick wit and open smile had added a new, surprising dimension to her life. "The heart can still somersault a bit," she had confessed.

Po and Max drove the short ride to Eleanor's house in comfortable silence, speaking only when the lights from the large three-story house on the corner of the campus lit up the night.

Murder on a Starry Night

"Looks like a full house," Max observed as they drove up the long circle drive.

"You know Eleanor—no matter how small the occasion, she doesn't want anyone to feel left out." Although tonight's event was officially a college function, Eleanor never hesitated to add her own guest list to the official one when she was opening the doors of Canterbury House for the event. And with one of the honorees this evening being Jedson Fellers the crowd was colorful, eclectic, and noisy. Max pulled his car into a small space near the curve of the driveway, and they followed the strains of a small jazz combo playing a medley of old Ray Charles tunes.

Max and Po walked through the open doorway and spotted Kate and P. J., standing in the spacious living room off the front hall, talking with Jed Fellers. Kate waved them over.

Her cheeks were bright and pink, and a pair of two-inch heels brought her nearly eye-to-eye with P.J. and Jed. A slight black dress of no discernible design floated over Kate's body with style and grace and looked like something straight off a designer's runway.

And she probably bought it at a thrift store for two dollars, Po thought, swallowing the pleasure that being Kate's godmother brought her on a continuous basis. Po hugged the tall, lanky professor standing beside her, looking every bit the part in a corduroy jacket with leather patches on the sleeves. "Congratulations, Jed," Po smiled. "What a treat, seeing you twice in one day."

"Thanks for coming, Po. You, too, Max. It was nice of the college and Eleanor to do this—it's great to see old friends."

"Eleanor loves an excuse for a party. And this is a nice excuse," Po said. "Sounds like the pressure is on at the university to publish. And you've survived the race, Jed."

Jed's book, entitled *A Plain Man's Guide to A Starry Night,* had received critical acclaim.

Jed nodded. "It gets crazy, that's for sure. It's just a little book. The fuss is unmerited."

"Well, big or little, it will be nice to have the university's publishing pressure off your back for awhile."

"Here, here," said Jed, lifting his glass.

"Gus Schuette had a couple copies in his store," P.J. said. He stood just behind Kate, one hand looped lightly around her shoulder. "It looked interesting. Astronomy has always been a secret passion of mine."

"Oh?" Kate turned her head and looked up into P.J.'s face. Her brows lifted. "A passion?"

"Well, secondary passion," P.J. said. He grinned at Kate. "You'll always be the primary P, Katie." P.J. tugged lightly on a loose strand of Kate's hair.

"Ah, my friends are here," Eleanor said, coming up behind the professor. "Good. Sometimes the university crew is a little boring." She kissed Jed on the cheek. "You excluded, my dear."

"*I think* that's a compliment," Jed said. "El, you're nice to do this."

"Pshaw with nice. I love it. It's a chance to be merry. We needed a diversion, Jed, and you and your friends are it."

"Diversion from what?" Jed asked.

"All this uproar over Adele Harrington and the house everyone and his brother seem to want." Eleanor waved to an old friend walking in the door.

"That commotion over the Harrington house is a curious thing," Max said. "Folks have disagreed with property sales and zoning laws before, but this is out of proportion. Sure, there's a lot of money at stake—but the land belongs to Adele Harrington, clean and clear. Tom Adler over at Prairie Development had me check—he claims Oliver promised to sell the house to him for a development. Says he saw the paper himself."

"Tom Adler?" Kate said. She accepted a piece of crisp, buttery toast topped with a sliver of rare tuna from a passing waiter.

"Adler claims Oliver wrote it out, like a will. Ollie didn't want Adele to get the house, according to Tom, and they were going to sign an agreement that would allow Oliver to live in the house free and clear as long as he liked, then Tom would take it over. Tom claims someone should check more closely into how Oliver died."

Po listened to the conversation around her silently. But her thoughts returned to Halley Peterson and the sentiment Po had dismissed as the voice of grief. *Oliver didn't die from a fall down the stairs*, she had implied.

"That matches some calls we've gotten at the station," P.J. was saying beside her. The tall, sandy-haired detective had returned to the group carrying a tray of champagne. "Anonymous callers have suggested there was foul play at the Harrington place. One caller went so far as to say the police must be on the take or they'd have looked into Oliver's death."

"That's odd," Eleanor said. "Didn't the papers say it was a heart attack?"

"That's the official word," P.J. said. "And it will hold until there's reason to think otherwise." P.J. pulled his vibrating cell phone out of his pocket, glanced at the number on the small screen, and looked up. "Sorry folks, duty calls." He moved over into a quiet corner to take the call.

Another waiter passed by, carrying a platter of chicken satay with a crystal cup filled with gingery peanut sauce. Small plates were passed around, and the group quickly emptied the tray.

"Eleanor, you certainly know how to throw a party," Kate said, balancing her plate in one hand and sipping her champagne. "This is terrific."

"The house should be used this way. One old soul doesn't do justice to this home," Eleanor said. "It was what old grandpop Harrison intended."

Eleanor's grandfather, Harrison Canterbury, had built the home over a hundred years before when he had moved his family from the east to the small Kansas town. A much better place to raise kids, he had decided. And having inherited a fortune as a railroad baron's son, he soon built Crestwood a bank, a department store, a church, and prettied up the city with several parks. But once his children started school, Harrison decided that what the town really needed was a college, and so he built one, right in the family's wooded backyard. Though the home was Eleanor's until she died, she was generous in opening it up for college events.

"Well, I'll be," Kate said, pausing between bites to stare at the front door. "Look who's here."

Po glanced over at the front door. The double doors were left open for the comings and goings of the guests. When an older professor whom Po had known for several decades walked with his wife out onto the portico, the view cleared.

Adele Harrington was alone, standing tall and elegant in a periwinkle silk dress. Her hair was down, falling loosely about her shoulders and held back from her face by an ebony comb. It was a transformation that drew unintentional sounds from Kate and Po. "Wow," Kate whispered. "What happened to the wicked witch of the north?"

Though not beautiful in a traditional sense, Adele was striking, her imposing manner heightened by the careful make-up and clothing. She stood alone, like an actor on a stage looking out over her audience.

"I don't think she was on the list, but it's certainly fine," Eleanor said. "Everyone is welcome to these things."

At that moment, Adele spotted the group, nodded in their direction, and walked into the living room. "Hello, everyone," she said. "Po, Kate, Max. And you, too, Eleanor, what a lovely party."

"Good evening, Adele," Eleanor said, and she looked toward Jed. "Do you know Professor Jed Fellers?"
Jed shook Adele's hand and bowed slightly.

Adele scrutinized him carefully, then said, "We met once."

"When Ollie won the award for his essay," Jed said. "I remember. What I remember especially is how happy he was that you came."

Adele was silent, but Po watched from the side as the words registered in Adele's mind and were stored away.

Anything she had done to make Ollie happy was important to her. Jed had said the right thing.

"I'm so sorry for your loss, Adele," Jed continued. "I'll miss your brother. He was a student of mine, but really more than that. Ollie was an inspiration to my students. He added much to my class." Jed paused, and when he spoke again, his voice was husky. "Ollie was my friend."

"Yes, I know that," Adele said. Her voice softened slightly. And then she turned back toward Eleanor. "My invitation must have been lost in the mail, Eleanor, being new in town and all. But I decided to come and see what all the fuss was about." She smiled carefully. "You don't mind, do you?"

"Of course not, Adele," Eleanor said, and stopped a passing couple to introduce them to the newly arrived guest.

"Where's P.J.?" Kate whispered to Po.

Po shrugged, but at that moment, P.J. wove his way through the crowded room and came up behind them. He rested one hand on Kate's shoulder, kneading it lightly.

Kate's smile faded when she looked into the concern clouding his face. "P.J., what's wrong?"

"I've bad news," he said softly. "The rumor mill seems to be right this time. Ollie Harrington didn't die from a fall. He was poisoned. It was in some tea he drank, apparently."

Just behind P.J., Adele Harrington stiffened at the sound of her brother's name. And then, in a fraction of a second, her strong shoulders sagged, and her carefully held body seemed to cave in on itself as she sank dramatically and directly, folding up like a rag doll in the center of Eleanor's thick crimson Gabbeh rug.

Murder on a Starry Night

CHAPTER 7

The gossip surrounding Adele Harrington's new bed and breakfast paled in the wake of the news that Oliver Harrington was murdered.

"Poor Adele," Selma Parker said, smoothing out a stretch of fabric on her cutting table. It was Tuesday afternoon and a welcome quiet settled down on the rows of colorful fabric in her fabric store. "Much as she annoys me, this must be a blow to her."

Po watched Selma cut into the deep blue fabric. She'd chosen Ollie's room as her project, and was honoring

Adele's request that the quilt be filled with stars. She had found a wonderful pattern in the *Kansas City Star* collection—one that combined a multitude of stars of every shape and form.

It was perfect, she decided, to honor the memory of a man who knew all kinds of stars—and who knew them intimately. She'd picked small patterns in blues and golds, rusts and deep, rich greens to make the quilt come to life in the small clean room that had been Ollie's.

"Po, these fabrics are going to look great." Selma folded the fabric pieces into a neat pile and slipped them into a sack. "How do you think Adele is doing?"

Po handed Selma her credit card. "All right, I think. Max and I took her home after she fainted the other night. By the time we got her inside and gave her a shot of brandy, she was clear-thinking and suggested strongly that we leave. I think she's denying this last bit of horrible news. She joked about crashing a party—then having it crash her. Something like that."

"Gutsy gal," Selma said. "I suppose I shouldn't be concerned about her."

"Well, she appears strong on the surface anyway."

Susan walked over to the checkout counter. "Have the police learned anything more? Rumors are rampant. I stopped at Marla's bakery this morning for a muffin and the buzz was as thick as that syrup she puts on her blueberry pancakes."

Po shook her head. "Marla thrives on all that. I'm sure she has the crime solved and wrapped up in a blue ribbon.

I don't think the official news is quite so clear-cut."

"Has P.J. said anything?" Susan asked.

"He was over for Sunday supper last night with Kate. It's kind of a mess, he said. All the work being done on the house has made it impossible to get any kind of prints—though the police have been questioning neighbors and others who had access to Ollie's house. There wasn't heavy traffic in that house, but repair men came and went, and old Joe Bates worked out there in the garden every day of Ollie's life, I think. He will certainly be questioned."

"Joe was devoted to Ollie. Maybe he'll shed some light on all this, though he doesn't hear so well anymore."

"I can't imagine anyone wanting to hurt that sweet man," Susan said. "I used to talk to him sometimes in between my weaving classes at the college. If he wasn't sitting in on a class, he was almost always in the library or in the commons, writing on his yellow pads."

"What did he write about?" Po asked.

"I don't know—things he learned in class, I guess. He hung on every word that came out of Professor Fellers' mouth. He was a true mentor to Ollie, and encouraged his love for learning new things. Ollie loved those classes. And if you ask me, he loved that librarian, too."

Po's head jerked up. "Halley Peterson?"

"Yes, that's her name—Halley. Nice person. She's worked in the library for a while now. Takes some classes, too. And she and Ollie were friends."

"I met her," Po said, and repeated the brief conversation she'd had with Halley. "At the time, I thought she was working through the natural emotions when someone dies—reaching out for answers and trying to make sense of such a sad happening. I thought lashing out at Adele was maybe her way of dealing with things."

The bell at Selma's front door jingled as several customers walked in. Selma looked over at them, then handed back Po's credit card. "We need to talk about this more," she said. "As I said, Adele Harrington isn't my favorite person, but I can't imagine she had anything to do with Ollie's death. She didn't show her face around here until his body was already in the morgue. And besides that, he was her twin brother, for heaven's sake. But I've already heard rumors of her wanting to get her hands on the house." Selma shook her head and walked off to help a young woman find some Irish lace.

"What do you think, Po?" Susan asked, her brow furrowed.

"I think this town doesn't need another lingering crime on its hands. I think the police need to solve this immediately, if not sooner. And frankly, I agree completely with Selma. I can't imagine that Adele Harrington had a thing to do with it."

"The rumors certainly aren't going to help her bed and breakfast business any."

Po nodded. "No, they're not. And that's a shame, too. So let's hope the crime is solved soon and we can all return to things as usual."

Po left the shop and walked down Elderberry Road toward Marla's bakery, thinking some sourdough rolls would be a nice complement to the cucumber and chicken soup she had planned for dinner. Perhaps Max would stop by, as he was prone to do lately, wandering in the back door and lifting the lid off the pot, wondering hungrily if there was enough for two. Of course he knew that Po never cooked for less than a family. It was her way, she always said. And somehow, miraculously, the food never went to waste.

A rapping on the window as she passed Picasso's French Quarter drew her out of her culinary thoughts, and Po smiled into the pleasant face of Max himself, looking out at her from the paned windows. He motioned for her to join him, then held up a half-empty glass. Po glanced at her watch—it was after five. A pre-dinner martini might just hit the spot, she thought, and turned toward the wide glass doors of the restaurant.

Picasso's bistro was a favorite gathering place for the entire neighborhood, and the Queen Bees quilters often stopped in for light lunches or dinner, especially when Picasso was serving his famous bouillabaisse. The food was a definite lure—fresh, flavorful fish and spices—but the round-faced chef was even more of a draw. Picasso St. Pierre had become a good and loyal friend.

The dining area of the bistro was separated from the bar by a row of plants and small cocktail tables. Today, at the table nearest the windows, P.J. and Jedson Fellers sat in spirited discussion while Max stood, a chair held back for Po.

"Good timing, Po," Max said, and motioned to the bartender to fix Po a martini, the way she liked it—up with an olive.

"Well, how nice is this? A martini at Picasso's and three handsome men. What more could a woman ask for?" Po set her purse on the floor and looked around the table. "What brings you three here. Have I interrupted something?" she asked.

"Nope," P.J. answered. "We were thinking we needed a woman's voice in this group, and who should walk by but yourself."

"Fate," Max said.

"Serendipity," Jed added.

"And what's the topic?" Po said, smiling at the young waiter who set her chilled martini glass down in front of her. She looked at P.J. and frowned. "You look serious, P.J. Has anything happened?"

"Nope." P.J. took her hand and squeezed it. Po was like a mother to him. She'd been in his family's life as long as he could remember. And now that he and Kate were an "item," as Po and her friends called it, Po was even more vigilant, watching over him and Kate with great care. "A chunk of change was given to Canterbury University in memory of Ollie, and they've decided to establish a scholarship fund in his name. The chancellor has asked Jed here to get involved since it will be awarded to a student in astronomy." P.J. nodded to Max. "And Max is the legal and numbers guy who's setting it up."

"And P.J., as a new board member over there, somehow got saddled with making it happen," Max added.

"That's a nice idea," Po said. "And I'm sure it'll mean a lot to Adele, especially with all this ugliness surrounding her life right now."

"Ollie deserves this honor," Jed said. "But I think Adele Harrington just wants all this put to rest. And I can understand that."

Po rested one hand on Jed's sleeve. If she was guessing correctly, this was almost as hard on Jed as it was on Adele. Even though Ollie was only a handful of years younger than Jed, Jed had been his mentor, a kind of father figure, and Po could see the grief in the professor's kind eyes.

"Adele doesn't believe Ollie was murdered," P.J. said. "She isn't being very cooperative in the investigation."

Po sipped her martini and listened to the men talk about the scholarship details. She could understand Adele's feelings. Murder was so ugly. Ollie was dead. There wasn't anything anyone could do about that. So let him rest. But the facts were what they were. And someone, as outlandish as it was, had ended Oliver's life far too early.

Po looked around the small, intimate bistro while the men continued to discuss the details of the scholarship fund. A crowd was gathering as folks stopped in after work for a drink and Picasso's amazing truffles. The buttery aroma of escargot filled the air, and she watched Picasso place the platter in front of Tom Adler and his curvaceous new wife, Cindy. Picasso loved the drama of his food, and he set it down with a flourish, his red face beaming with delight over his prize appetizer.

He caught Po's eye, winked, and soon edged his way over to her table, greeting customers on his way. "My magnificent Po," he said, kissing her lightly on each cheek. Then straightening up and looking into her eyes. "Such talk, mon amie, all over my restaurant tonight. All about Ollie Harrington."

"Has Tom Adler settled down any?" Po nodded toward the man now relishing the platter of snails.

"Non, no, no. He is so upset, Po. Says he wasn't the one who killed Ollie, but just maybe he knows who did. And then he said some awful things about Ollie's twin sister."

P.J., Jed, and Max stopped talking and looked at Picasso.

"I know Adler is pretty crazed about all this," P.J. said. "He'd been in the station a couple of times, begging the police to stop Adele's renovations. He claims the land is his. Ollie promised him that when he died, he could have it, he says. And he says there's a piece of paper somewhere in that house that confirms his claims. But Adele won't let him past the front door, of course."

Po took a sip of her martini and looked over at Tom over the rim. "I'd suggest he watch his rantings," she said. "It seems to me that's a likely murder motive."

"His company isn't doing too well," Max said. "Developing the Harrington property would put him back on his feet. But I can't imagine why Ollie would give it to him."

Picasso nodded. He dropped his voice to avoid being heard beyond their table. "He pestered Oliver all the time, that much I saw myself. He even brought him in here once or twice and tried to get him drinking, but Ollie didn't ever touch a drop. Not once. Oliver's only libations were milk and tea. Tea and my escargot," Picasso said, his eyes rolling and one hand slapping a round, red cheek. "My mama would turn over in her grave."

Po had seen Ollie in Picasso's once or twice—and a few

other places on Elderberry Road—picking up cheese at Jess and Ambrose's Brew and Brie—but most often at Gus Schuette's bookstore where he'd sometimes come in with Jed and the two men would sit for hours over a round table in the back of the bookstore, discussing the galaxies and new stars. The thought of anyone wanting that quiet man dead was almost beyond comprehension. Unless, of course, someone had something very important to gain by his death.

Po looked over at Tom Adler while she sipped her drink. He was talking heatedly with someone from the city council, shaking his head, then waving his hands in the air. He'd had a few drinks, Po could tell, and it wasn't helping his composure any. But she'd known Tom long enough to know his bark was stronger than his bite. Or so she'd always thought. Next to him, his wife looked bored and seemed to be entertaining herself by admiring the large diamonds decorating her fingers.

Catching Po's look, Tom nodded at her, forcing a slight smile to his face. A few minutes later, he slapped down a few bills, and he and his bride left the bistro abruptly, brushing aside a young waiter as they hurried through the door.

Po watched him through the window. Tom and Cindy crossed Elderberry Road, barely noticing a car that nearly sideswiped them, then climbed into a big truck parked in front of Max's law office. Gravel shot out from under the tires as he tore off down the street.

That anger can only come to no good, Po thought. It isn't a healthy thing.

"Mon Dieu!" Picasso said beside her, and startled Po

from her thoughts. But he wasn't watching Tom's hasty exit; he was staring at the front door.

Po followed his look. Adele Harrington stood just inside the door, her hair uncharacteristically mussed, her hands on her hips. Her face was a mixture of anger and determination, and her eyes immediately settled in on Po.

"Po Paltrow," Adele called out across the crowded room, "I need to talk to you. Immediately, if you don't mind."

CHAPTER 8

"Adele." Po was out of her chair in seconds. She had recently helped pick Adele's crumbled form up from a floor, and she didn't want to risk that happening in Picasso's crowded bistro. The disgrace would be too heavy for Adele to bear. "Are you all right?" Po asked, reaching her side.

Adele was dressed perfectly as always, in tailored slacks and a fine cashmere sweater. A red silk jacket warded off the fall chill. But her face lacked its characteristic composure. The mask that hid all emotion was gone and her eyes blazed. "No, Portia, I am not fine. Would you and P.J. please come with me."

Po turned toward the table and gestured to P.J. to join her. The two looked apologetically at a confused Max and Jed and followed Adele outside.

Adele stood beneath Picasso's blue awning and took in a deep, stabilizing breath. "Someone," she said at last, "has been in my house."

Po looked at Adele silently, wondering if she had been pushed, at last, to the edge.

P.J said, "Adele, there are dozens of people in your house every day."

Adele cast him an annoyed look. "Someone," she said, dismissing P.J.'s comment with a clipped tone, "broke into my house during the night. Paint was spilled, furniture was damaged. Someone evil is trying to prevent my bed and breakfast from opening on time."

"Are you sure it wasn't a workman's error?" Po asked. "Paint could easily have been spilled."

"Please, spare me," Adele said. "I said that someone is breaking the law. You are the law, are you not?" She glared at P.J.

"Have you called the police?" P.J. asked. "There are police assigned to this case, Adele, and they—"

Adele held out her hands to quiet him. "I wanted to talk with someone I know personally. Police can be so annoying. I called Kate Simpson, and she told me I would find you here. Now, what are we going to do about this?"

"Was anything taken?"

"Not that I could tell. But how would I know? The house is a mess. Things everywhere."

"I'll see that someone comes out to investigate the damage, Adele, and you'll have to file a report," P.J. said.

"No. What I want is for this to stop, P.J. Flanigan. I have felt for several days that things were not right in the house. Things were askew. Moved around. I have kept many family things intact all through the house to create ambiance. Things have been disturbed, I could feel it."

"Were you in the house last night, Adele?" Po asked. "Did you hear anything?"

"I wasn't there. The paint smell had been disturbing my sleep so I was staying at that Canterbury Inn on campus. But I won't do that again. I would certainly have heard the vandals and put a stop to it."

P.J. listened, his thoughts moving back to the night before. It had been one of those near-perfect, Indian summer nights, and he and Kate had taken a late-night walk beneath a deep canopy of stars. They'd stopped for sushi at a new little restaurant near the river, filled with college students taking a break from cramming for mid-terms—and then they had walked back through the Elderberry neighborhood and down Kingfish Drive. Adele's home had been quiet, he remembered, because they had paused to admire the gardens freshly tilled along the drive. They were lit by a row of low lights that Adele had recently installed beneath the new plantings. The big stone house loomed large in the background, lit softly with security lights and the stars from above. The only inside lights they could see came from the back garage apartment that Joe Bates lived in. And while they stood at the end of the drive, those lights went out, too, and they saw Joe come out of the apartment and light up a cigar beside the garage. At risk of disturbing his privacy, they had walked on down the street.

"We walked by your house last night, Adele," P.J. said aloud. "It was quiet."

"I don't care about quiet," Adele snapped. "Sometime, somehow, someone did damage inside my house, and it must stop. You are the police, do something."

"Joe Bates was there. He may have heard something. Have you talked with him?"

"Joe Bates is a fool. Always has been. And as soon as I can figure out a way to get rid of him, I will do so. My mother and then my brother took pity on him and gave him a home there—."

"He's a wonderful gardener, Adele," Po said. Joe had done work for her over the years and everything the man touched turned to beauty. Po liked Joe, and wondered at Adele's disdain for such a gentle, old man who wouldn't hurt a fly.

"He's another piece of Oliver's life, which is now gone," Adele said. "He doesn't deserve to be here and have my brother be gone." And then she spun around on heels Po wouldn't dream of wearing, even to an elegant party, and she and P.J. watched in silence as Adele walked across the street to her Cadillac.

Adele paused beside the car and looked back at Po and P.J. "I'm not a fool, Po Paltrow," she called across the street. "I am very aware that there are people in this town who, No. 1, want me out of here, and No. 2, want my property.

But neither of those things are going to happen. And I will prosecute anyone who stands in my way." She slipped behind the wheel, and in the next minute, she was gone, driving far too fast for a quiet evening.

Po shook her head. "Poor Adele. There's something very sad about that woman."

"Nasty, is more like it," P.J. said. He shoved his hands in his jeans' pockets and looked up at the sky. "I think I need something really nice to get rid of the taste."

"Like Kate?" Po asked, eyebrows lifting playfully.

P.J. laughed. "Now you're a mind reader, Po. Scary."

"Will you follow-up on Adele's claims?"

He nodded. "I'll make a call to the station and have someone go out to the house. And then I think I'll see if Katie has any of her grilled salmon and orzo salad lying around looking for someone to eat it."

Po laughed and looked up into P.J.'s clear blue eyes. They were quite bright these days, she thought. Happy eyes. And that made Po happy, too. And Po's best friend Liz would be delighted—delighted and pleased that her spirited daughter—who didn't always follow the rules—had found someone as wonderful as P.J. Flanigan.

"Think you can handle the men in there by yourself?" P.J. nodded toward the bistro window where Max now stood, peering out, a puzzled look on his face.

"Of course I can, P.J." Po said. "Give Kate my love, and I'll talk with you tomorrow. I'd like to know if there is any truth to Adele's story." She waved him off and slipped back into the bistro, wondering if Jed Fellers

Murder on a Starry Night

had somewhere he had to be. Two could play at P.J.'s game—a nice homemade pasta with Max, a martini on the deck, and a chance to talk with a close friend might fill the evening's bill nicely.

And it might also ease the nagging feeling she had that things were truly not right at 210 Kingfish Drive— and that they'd be hearing more, not less, of Adele's bed and breakfast in the days to come.

CHAPTER 9

"What do you think, ladies?" Phoebe held up a finished block for her quilt.

"Phoebe, that's wonderful!" Kate set her coffee cup down and leaned across the table to see the colorful green and pink flowered block. Phoebe was using the butterfly pattern from one of the *Kansas City Star's* quilt books. She'd chosen playful calico prints in pink, bright reds, greens and yellows.

"I think it's pretty cool myself," Phoebe said.

"Adele wanted at least one crib quilt. That was thoughtful of her, don't you think?" Selma said. "And Phoebe is the perfect person to make it."

"Perfect, hah. Jimmy is getting worried. We're about to move Jude and Emma into youth beds, and Jimmy knows it's painful for me to have an empty crib in the house. When he saw me working on this block he like freaked. He turned as white as Eleanor's hair."

Eleanor laughed and patted Phoebe's hand. "You are a good mom, Phoebe dear. You should have twenty little ones."

"Twenty little what?" Susan asked, coming through the archway into the back room of Selma's store.

"Phoebe's deciding her future," Po said. "And while she does, let's see your quilt, Susan. It's for that gigantic king-sized bed in the tower suite, right?"

Susan opened a cabinet and pulled out a stack of finished blocks. The pile of colors—yellow gold, greens, silvery blues and grays, and deep pinks—was remarkable, even without being set in a design. "Adele wanted something different in that room—something contemporary—so I didn't use a traditional pattern."

"Susan, you could scatter those colors on a bed just like they are and you'd create a beautiful tapestry," Po said, admiring the kaleidoscope of color.

Susan smoothed out one of the blocks. "Adele—believe it or not—had a trunk filled with gorgeous silk fabrics. She'd collected them from her travels all over the world. We went through it together and I pulled these out for the quilt."

Selma stood next to Susan and looked closely at the design sketched on the piece of paper. "I think people will pay to stay in this room for the quilt alone. It's gorgeous, honey."

The border would be strips of gray and blue pieced together, and in the center was a vibrant swirl of pink, spiraling out into yellows and golds. It was all movement and color. "I went over to check the paint color and figure out the border last night. The house is really coming along," Susan said. "Kate went to keep me company."

"To nose around is more like it," Kate said. "The Harrington house fascinates me. It always did, even when I was little, though it frightened me back then. The Harringtons were so private. And after his parents died, Ollie sometimes let the house go, with weeds all over. It reminded me of Boo Radley's house in *To Kill a Mockingbird*—frightening and mysterious—but holding something decent. And now the house is beautiful, but that something decent is missing. And no one seems to know why. It's sad. And unnerving, and until the murderer is caught, the real beauty of that house can't come through. It just can't."

"Kate," Po said. The single word was a warning, and everyone in the room could hear it in Po's soft tone.

"There's no danger, Po," Susan said.

"Someone has been murdered, Susan. We can't take that lightly."

"But don't you suspect it's someone far removed from us—and probably not from Crestwood?" Susan said. "And whoever did it is a world away by now. The life Ollie lived here was such an ordinary one. It had to be someone distant, maybe someone from another part of the Harringtons' life—"

"Susan, you're dreaming," Eleanor said. "There are a half dozen people within a mile of here who might have killed Ollie—and in his or her own twisted mind, had reason to do it."

"And it's usually the guy next door. The one you least expect," Phoebe added enthusiastically. "Gus Schuette gave me a book to read on murder motives, and it's not complicated at all. It's pretty much for love or lust or money."

Kate laughed. "Phoebe, what are you reading books on murder motives for?"

"Someone has to solve this crime," Phoebe replied. "No offense against P.J. and his buds, Kate, but I don't see anyone being arrested. And if we don't clear this all up before Adele's grand opening next month, there will be no one making reservations in that bed and breakfast. And that means no one will see these works of art we're rushing to the finish line."

"The crime will be solved," Po said confidently. "And by the police, not us, not Kate or Phoebe rushing in to do heaven knows what." But deep down Po didn't feel confident at all. Adele Harrington lived just a few blocks from her home, and the same distance from Kate's. Phoebe's apprehension was credible. Even when the trouble wasn't being talked about, it was there in the background of their lives—the awful fact that there might be someone in their midst who was capable of killing a kind, gentle man. And until that someone was found, the restlessness would remain.

"On a brighter spot, where's our Maggie?" Eleanor asked.

"Funny, I talked with her last night. She was definitely going to be here to show off the progress on her quilt," Kate said.

Po frowned. "I hope that rattletrap truck of hers didn't break down on the way over."

Kate laughed. "I think Mags keeps that truck as a sign of her independence." A few years before, Maggie's then-husband had almost bankrupted her clinic, whittling away at her money on weekend junkets to Las Vegas. The truck was one of the few things Maggie didn't lose. But through hard work and with the help of good friends, she now had one of the most successful veterinary clinics in Kansas.

The sound of wheels on gravel in the alley running behind the Elderberry shops broke into the conversation, and in the next minute, Maggie's truck pulled up to the back door, and she burst into the room. In place of her usual smile was a worried, disturbed look.

"Maggie, what's wrong?" Po asked.

Maggie sat down and rested her elbows on her knees. "It's Emerson," she said.

"The poet?" Eleanor asked, handing Maggie a cup of coffee.

"Adele's dog," Po said, suddenly understanding Maggie's lateness. An emergency. "Is Emerson all right?"

"Someone tried to poison him," Maggie said.

CHAPTER 10

The quilting group disbanded shortly after hearing Maggie's news. But Po had not been able to concentrate on much of anything for the rest of the day. Her books lay stacked on the desk, unopened. Her computer silent. And the diminishing daylight cast a chill that even a hot cup of tea couldn't dispel.

A quick phone call to Max convinced him he needed to spend time on Po's deck that evening.

"First Oliver's death. And now a dog being poisoned. Max, what is going on here?" Po handed Max an icy martini, then wrapped a thick wool sweater around her shoulders and sat down next to him on her back deck settee. She had related the terrible story of Emerson's poisoning in full detail, down to the good news, that Emerson would be able to come home that same day, relieving Adele of the worry of being without him for even a night.

Max looked off into the deepening night. The flicker of small spotlights beneath the towering trees cast shadows across the deep backyard. Max stretched his legs out and sipped the martini. "It's not good, Po, that's for sure. I dropped some estate papers off for her this afternoon so she didn't have to come down to the office. Emerson is sleepy, but otherwise he'll be fine."

Po nodded. It was kind of Max to stop by. Maggie said Emerson was weak from the effects of the poison. And Adele would want to be there with him and not visiting a lawyer's office. Absently, as if directed by thoughts of a dog, Po reached down and scratched Hoover's ears. Her ancient Irish Setter thumped his tail in thanks.

"How was Adele?" Po asked.

"She was pure Adele. Always wanting to appear in command. But she loves that dog—and she's convinced it's evil doing, as she put it. She tosses out names of possible culprits without a second thought. It's a long list, let me tell you. Everyone from Tom Adler, to neighbors, to the president of the college board. People who want to scare her into leaving town."

"That's so awful. I know she's suspicious of Joe Bates, too, but that's probably just an excuse to urge him to find another place to live."

"Well, she can't force Joe out. It's in Oliver's will that Joe has a place there as long as he wants it. It was Adele's mother's wish as well."

"I'm sure that irritates Adele. She doesn't much like being told what she can and can't do."

Max laughed. "That's putting it mildly, Po. She's got quite a temper, that one."

Po took another sip of her martini and thought about Adele's life—or the little she knew of it. She'd gone back east to college, then traveled all over the world as a representative of a pharmaceutical company. She made plenty of money, from all accounts. Selma heard that she might have been married briefly, but no one knew for sure. And now here she was, back in Crestwood, Kansas, opening up a bed and breakfast. And turning neighbors and others against her with dizzying speed. "Sometimes I think Adele is all sound and fury," Po said.

"Signifying nothing?"

"No. Maybe something. Perhaps a vulnerability—a fear of being hurt. If you push everyone away, no one is likely to hurt you."

"Well, it isn't working," Max said. "I think this thing with Emerson is hurting her."

Po nodded. Of course Adele was hurting, Max was right. "And surely she suffers greatly from the loss of her only sibling, though she manages to keep her feelings under lock and key." A breeze rustled through the branches and Po looked up beyond the trees, into a glorious fall sky. The stars were abundant tonight, filling the black vastness with a brightness that belied the cloud hanging over Crestwood. She reached for Max's hand and felt his fingers comfortably wind through her own. Her own hand was icy from the martini glass, but Max's was warm. Warm and comforting.

Max looked over at her and smiled. "Po, this mess will be solved, you know. And soon, I think. Peace will return."

Po rested her head on his shoulder. Yes, it would pass and the cloud would lift. The Harrington House at 210 Kingfish Drive would open to fine reviews. But between now and then, Po suspected life wouldn't be the same at all. And she wondered to herself how many lives would be touched in that interlude.

The ringing of the telephone scattered Po's thoughts. "I'll get it," she said to Max, rising from the couch. For a moment her heart beat too fast, and she stood still beside the deck swing listening to the night sounds. And for that instance, Po didn't want to answer the phone at all. The news, she knew instinctively, would not be good.

CHAPTER 11

Po walked into the kitchen and picked up the phone. It was Kate, her voice high and her words coming out too quickly.

Po's heart skipped a beat. Since Kate's mother's death, Po had assumed the same role with Kate that she had with her own three children—fearing, when the phone rings late at night, that her child might be hurt.

"Kate, what is it?"

"Oh, Po, when is this craziness going to end? P.J. and I were out on our bikes tonight, riding along the river, getting something to eat. Then—"

"Kate," Po stopped her, her knuckles white against the receiver. "Are you all right? P.J.?"

"Yes, Po," Kate said, impatient to get on with her story. "Everyone you love is fine. But there are others in Crestwood not so fine."

Po slowly released the air that was creating fire in her lungs. "Go on, sweetie."

"Well, we rode past the Harrington estate on the way back to my house, and as we were going around the corner, we heard sirens, then a police car, and then the emergency medical van spun around the corner and pulled into 210 Kingfish."

"So you and P.J. followed."

"P.J. thought he could help."

"Of course."

Kate went on. "Adele Harrington was standing out in the driveway in her nightgown, though it was only nine or so. And Halley Peterson—that nice librarian from the college was there. And Joe Bates, the gardener."

"That's an odd threesome."

"Yes, I thought so, too."

Po could almost feel the adrenalin surging through Kate's body and wished, for a moment, that her goddaughter didn't love danger quite so much.

"Halley was in tears," Kate continued, "and Joe had blood gushing from his forehead."

"That poor man. Is he all right?"

"It was mostly superficial, P.J. said. Apparently Adele hit him with one of the workmen's tools because she thought he was breaking into her house, or so she said."

"And Adele called the police?"

"No, Halley did. She was walking up the drive and heard Joe scream, then saw the blood as he was trying to get back to the carriage house. So she called 911 from her cell phone."

"What was she coming to see Adele for at that hour? That's odd, especially since Adele isn't very fond of her." She felt Max standing close behind her and turned, assuring him with a smile that everything was okay. "Kate," she whispered, her hand cupping the receiver, then nodded toward the coffee brewing on the counter and the apple pie right beside it.

Max's brows lifted with pleasure. He walked over and helped himself to a generous slice, then settled down at Po's table with Hoover at his side.

"I don't know why Halley was there," Kate answered. "Things were a little crazy, as you can imagine. Adele was upset that the police came. She said she could handle things herself."

"Did she bring charges against Joe?"

"No. She wanted everyone to go home and forget the whole thing happened. Which they did, but of course the police had to file a report of the call."

"What happened then?"

"It was kind of anticlimactic. Adele went inside. Joe shuffled off to his carriage house with a bandaged head, and Halley kind of disappeared. I really don't know where she went.

"P.J. talked to the fellows from the department for a

few minutes—they thought the whole thing was strange. Adele's actions and the whole uncooperative way she's treated Ollie's death and murder have the police on alert. She isn't above suspicion, P.J. says. She only has the house because Ollie died, so there's motive. And things like this don't help the way they think about her."

"Was Joe actually breaking in?"

"Well, turns out he has a key, so no, he wasn't exactly breaking in. Adele heard a sound coming from the back door, picked up a hammer a workman had left and really hit him hard with it. She could have hurt him badly. Fortunately the paramedics came to check him out, and they said he'd be fine."

"Adele isn't crazy about Joe, she's made that clear. But this isn't exactly the way to handle it. Why was he going into her kitchen?"

"He adopted Neptune, Ollie's cat, and he thought the cat had been locked inside the house. He didn't want the cat to have to spend the night with Adele, he said."

Po smiled. That sounded like Joe. He was always a bit crusty.

"He mumbled something to the police about Ollie's murder. Said they were looking in all the wrong places."

"That's strange."

"He wasn't talking very sensibly. And everyone thought he should go take some aspirin and go to bed. I think he'd had a few beers. He growled at Adele, then finally walked off, and I—" Kate paused.

"What?" Po asked, feeling Kate's unfinished thought.

"Po, I don't know why exactly, but for a moment, I felt sorry for Adele. She seemed vulnerable somehow, standing out on that driveway. She tried to put on her usual brave, brassy façade, but she couldn't quite pull it off. There was a crack in the stone."

Po listened, nodding. A few minutes later, with Kate's assurance that she was through with any detective work for the night, she hung up and sat beside Max at the table while he finished his second piece of pie. She filled him in on the pieces of the story he hadn't grasped from hearing one side of the conversation. The facts were unpleasant— and the thought of Adele swinging a hammer at old Joe Bates was an unforgiving one.

But beneath all the facts, Po suspected Kate was right. Adele's façade was crumbling. And she wasn't the ogre she wanted everyone to think she was. There was, indeed, a crack in the stone.

CHAPTER 12

Po had been trying to get to the Canterbury library for several days. Her excuse was to pick up another book Leah was holding for her and to do a little research. But the real reason was to talk to Halley Peterson again, to find out what in the world she was doing at the Harrington mansion late on a Saturday night.

A quick call to the library confirmed that Halley was working that day, and when Halley herself came to the phone, she agreed to meet Po for a cup of coffee around three. Po wasn't sure if she was reading into it or not, but she thought she heard relief in Halley's voice, or at the least, a desire to talk with Po.

Po threw a bright blue cotton sweater over her white blouse and jeans and walked the few blocks to the college. It was another amazing fall day with temperatures in the upper sixties, and everywhere Po looked, trees were turning into bouquets of color. The ugliness of Oliver's death hanging over the town was an aberration and didn't fit at all with the beauty around them. *Soon*, Po thought. *Please let it end soon.*

In ten minutes, Po reached the edge of campus and slowed down as she passed Eleanor's big house. Eleanor was like Joe Bates, she thought, admiring the large urns, filled to overflowing with crimson mums. The two of them just looked at a plant and it eagerly responded with beautiful blossoms. She'd have to remember to tell Eleanor how wonderful her home looked.

A bevy of coeds in shorts and t-shirts ran by, and Po stepped aside, admiring their speed and energy as they ran toward town. Her own jogs were not nearly so speedy, but they energized her just the same. And, she thought with a slight trace of pride, kept her in the same-sized jeans she'd worn thirty years ago.

Po walked beneath the large stone entrance arch and across the green area that centered the college. She loved the small campus and welcomed the flood of memories that warmed her from the inside out every time she walked the tree-lined lanes crisscrossing the campus. When Sam Paltrow had been president, Po stopped by nearly every day for one thing or another—to bring one of the kids by to see their dad, to have a little quiet time with her husband in his high-ceiling office in the administration building, to attend benefits and meetings. It was a second home, and Sam's early death hadn't changed that feeling—the faculty and staff considered her family and she always felt welcome here. She wondered briefly how Sam would feel about the difference in status, the college growing into a university. It was a matter of funding, she knew, simply semantics. But she resented the pressure it put on friends like Leah and Jed to have to publish articles and books to remain in good standing. It all seemed like a rather childish game to her.

Po greeted several faculty members as she walked past the theatre building and crossed over to the library on the other side of the quad. Inside the cool stone building, she was greeted by an enormous painting of her Sam, looking down at her from the paneled wall in the entryway. She nodded at him, smiling into his clear blue eyes. She let the catch in her breathing pass before moving on. Dear Sam. Always with her, but always, always, giving her permission to move on.

The library was busy with students cramming for exams. Po didn't see Halley behind the curved desk, but she was a bit early for their coffee date, so she headed for a computer to find her own titles.

A short while later, her yellow notepad filled with scribbles and two books checked out and slipped into her backpack, Po looked around for Halley. "Check the Hawthorne reading room," a young girl at the desk told her. "I think she was helping one of the professors with his reserved reading list."

Po thanked her and wound her way around a bank of carrels to a smaller room off a hallway. That room, too, was filled with students at library tables, heads bent together, books open between them, and a buzz in the air that spoke of pending exams.

Po spotted Halley over on the other side of the room, standing beside a carrel. She was talking softly to a man whose back was to Po. While she talked, she removed her glasses, then smiled shyly and leaned forward slightly to hear what the man was saying.

Po smiled as she watched the interaction. *She's flirting with him,* she thought with some surprise, then started to turn away, embarrassed to be eavesdropping on the librarian.

At that moment, Halley looked up and caught Po's eye. She gave her a small wave, said something to the man in the carrel, and hurried across the room, glancing up at the big clock on the wall.

"I'm so sorry, Po. I didn't realize the time."

"You were busy doing your job," Po said. "It's a little crazy around here."

"Yes," Halley said in a low voice. "Very crazy. Professors are trying to get reading lists lined up for the rest of the fall semester and the kids are cramming." With a sweep of her hand, she took in the crowded room. "Look at this, not an empty table in sight. But I love the activity."

Po noticed the sparkle in Halley's eyes, missing when she

was talking with Adele Harrington just days ago. Her cheeks were pink and glowing. "I can see you love what you do," she said, and followed Halley's gaze around the room.

"Yes," Halley said softly. "I love what I do. I get to take classes for free, I meet fascinating people, and I work in this amazing library. This is where I met Ollie."

"You miss him," Po said, reading the wistful sound in Halley's voice.

"I do. And lots of others do, too. He had friends here, people who loved him."

Po nodded. "I know that, Halley. And speaking of Ollie, shall we get that cup of coffee? I could certainly use one. And we can talk more about your friend Ollie, too."

Halley agreed, and began walking toward the door.

Po lifted her backpack over her shoulder and followed, glancing back briefly at the carrel in the back of the room and the man who seemed to have added a glow to Halley's cheeks.

At that moment, the man stood, picked up his briefcase, and turned to speak to a student asking his help.

Po smiled in surprise as she looked at the handsome profile of Jedson Fellers. Goodness, she thought, one never knew.

"A cup of coffee is exactly what I need to keep me going another couple of hours," Halley said as she and

Po settled in a booth in the small coffee shop that the college had recently constructed. It was a light and airy place with comfortable couches and chairs and a line of booths along one window.

"How long have you worked at Canterbury, Halley?" Po asked.

"Forever, it seems." Halley pushed a strand of loose brown hair behind her ear. "After a few years in the library, I started taking classes, so now I combine the two. The work, of course, makes the other possible—and the college is very generous to its employees."

Po nodded. Halley Peterson was a hard worker, which she suspected from the first time she saw her—a hard worker and a woman of purpose. Just going back to school when you were in your mid-thirties took some gumption. "And you and Ollie became friends here, you said?"

"Yes."

Halley's face was a mirror of her soul, Po thought as a range of emotions spread out from her eyes. Sorrow, colored with happy memories. Po understood the blend well.

"Ollie spent lots of time in the library when he wasn't in classes. Sometimes new students poked fun at him—he was so much older than they were—but before long they'd stop because so many of us knew him and liked him and once you talked to him, you saw the kindness in him. Professors let him sit in on classes, and he knew everyone. Jed Fellers, especially, took Ollie under his wing. But you probably know that. Jed was a mentor to Ollie, and then they became good friends." Halley paused and took a drink of coffee, her voice strained with emotion. For a moment, she and Po sat in silence, the memories of Ollie Harrington filling the space between them.

Halley wrapped her long narrow fingers around her coffee cup and went on. "Sometimes Jed and Ollie let me sit with them and listen when they'd talk about astrology, and a couple of times the three of us went down to the Powell observatory in Louisburg for their Starbright Saturday night programs. Ollie didn't go out much, but he loved going down there with the professor. Jed would explain to us what we were seeing, and then we'd go somewhere for coffee and talk about it all. Ollie would get so excited. He learned so much from Jed, and Jed would just sit there and beam at his prize student, so proud as Ollie waxed eloquently about all those things—the Pleiades cluster, the Andromeda galaxy, things I'd never heard about before."

"I didn't know about that part of Ollie's life, Halley. It makes me happy to know he had such special times with good friends."

Halley wiped the moisture from her eyes with the back of her hand. "Ollie loved those times, and he loved it at Canterbury," she said. "He used to tell me that Canterbury was his surrogate family And when I met his sister, I understood why he said that."

"You aren't fond of Adele," Po said.

"I don't know her that well," Halley answered, a slight trace of defensiveness in her voice.

"But you've talked, that I know."

"That was foolish of me. Sometimes I get involved where I don't belong, I guess. But I cared so much for him. Ollie even convinced me to take a class in astronomy last semester."

"From Jed?"

Halley blushed slightly. "Well, Ollie told me he was the best. And he was right."

"It's good Ollie's friends have each other now. That helps. I know when my Sam died, my friends at Canterbury were so important."

"Jed was mostly Ollie's friend. But since Ollie's death, he lets me talk about him, and we share lots of good memories. I can tell him how sad I feel and he understands. I told him how much it would mean to have something of Ollie's. And he encouraged me to let Adele know, so I did."

"Was it his telescope you wanted?" The telescope was clearly valuable, and Po could understand that Adele might be suspicious of someone she didn't know wanting to take it. That might explain Adele's anger toward Halley.

"Oh, no, not that. Telescopes you can *buy*, Po. I wanted to get some of Ollie's writings, some of his thoughts that he put in written form. Some books." She looked out the window, as if deciding how much to say to Po. When she turned back, her words were deliberate and careful. "Ollie talked sometimes about me sharing his home someday." Halley paused for a long time. When she spoke again, her voice was profoundly sad. "And then he was murdered. And no one seems to be doing much about it."

"The police are doing everything they can, Halley."

"Then why is Adele Harrington still building a bed and breakfast? Why is she still occupying that house, acting like everything's fine?"

"Do you think Adele had something to do with Ollie's death?" Po asked. A young waitress appeared and refilled their cups, then disappeared across the room.

"It's the only way she could get her hands on that property. I know Ollie wasn't going to will it to her. Adele never liked Crestwood—Ollie told me that. She doesn't deserve his home—he wanted someone to have it who would appreciate it."

"Someone like you."

"Or Joe Bates, or anyone who would care for it, not turn it into a way to make money."

"I heard what happened to Joe Bates the other night."

Halley's head shot up. "You know about that?"

Po nodded.

"Of course you do. Kate Simpson was there. And her boyfriend. I almost forgot."

"Why were you going to see Adele again? Was it for his things that you mentioned? I know she wasn't very receptive to you a couple weeks ago."

Halley laughed softly, but her face grew sad. "I wasn't there to see Adele. I was going to see Joe."

"Joe? So he was getting something in the house for you?" That would explain a lot of things. Perhaps Joe was the one who had entered the house a few nights ago, looking for things of Ollie's so they wouldn't be thrown away.

She shook her head. "No, Joe wasn't breaking into her

house. He wouldn't do that. He was just trying to get Neptune, like he told the police. Neptune was Ollie's cat, and he sometimes went back into the house, looking for Ollie. I had just arrived when it happened.

"Joe is terribly lonely now, and every now and then he calls me and asks me to come look through the telescope with him like he and Ollie did. Or look through some of Ollie's things that he'd confiscated from the trash pile that Adele was throwing out. He'd go through it every single day to be sure nothing of Ollie's was heaved into the dumpster.

"But the other night he was very upset when he called. He said I needed to come talk to him. He knew who killed Ollie, he said, and he could prove it if only I would help him find something."

Po frowned. "Find something?"

Halley smiled sadly. "Joe has been a little crazy since Ollie died. He's been obsessed with things, first about the house, who would get it. And lately he's called me a couple of times when he doesn't make sense. The other night he was particularly anxious, so I thought I had better go over and talk to him, make sure he was all right."

"So you think he was just ranting? Could he know something, do you think?"

Halley shook her head. "I don't know, Po. He loved Ollie so much, and he hasn't been quite himself since this happened. I think sometimes he feels guilty, like he should have kept Ollie from dying."

"That's a burden he shouldn't have to bear, Halley. Joe

has been with the family for a long time. Whenever I went to see Ollie, Joe would check me out, make sure he knew who I was. He was probably the best security guard Ollie could have had, not that he needed one. Joe rarely left the property since Mrs. Harrington died. I asked him once if he'd do some more yard work for me, and he told me he couldn't—his job was with Oliver. Ollie couldn't have asked for a more devoted friend."

Halley looked out the window again. Students wandered by alone and in groups, relishing the fall sunshine. Welcoming mid-term exams and a brief fall break from school. Finally she brought her attention back to Po. "Joe and Ollie were an odd couple, Ollie the brain, Joe the caretaker. Ollie said his mom made sure that Joe was always there for him."

"And Ollie's father? Did he ever talk about him?" Po had known Walter Harrington socially, but had always found him slightly unapproachable. Distant.

"No, he didn't talk much about his father. I don't think Mr. Harrington had much to do with his son. Ollie wasn't going to take over the family holdings or be the corporate leader his father was, so he didn't matter much, is the way I interpreted it. It was his mother Ollie cared about and who cared about him."

"I know when she was diagnosed with cancer a couple of years after Walter died, Ollie was bereft."

"He told me about that. Ollie was about my age when she died, I think."

Po nodded. "About that, maybe a little older. Ollie

became kind of a recluse for awhile, then sought out the college, and he seemed to find a life again."

"It's all so tragic. This sweet man. There was a brilliance beneath his simple surface, at least when it came to constellations and things like that. It was almost an obsession."

Po smiled. That was so true. She remembered how as a young boy, Ollie would come to her door, selling odds and ends he'd find around town so he could buy small binoculars or books about the stars. He'd tell her exactly where Mars was that day and what his favorite constellation was. And he was so happy when someone would listen to him.

"Why would anyone kill Ollie, Po?" Halley asked suddenly. "Is land that important? Did Adele want that house so badly? In the four years I've known Ollie, she visited him once. Once! And it was awful—she wanted Ollie to move into a small condominium near her and sell the house. Can you imagine Ollie in a condominium? It was an awful time for him. And now she's back and has what she wants. The estate is all hers. And she's turning it into something he wouldn't have liked at all."

"Maybe he'd have liked his sister coming home at last, Halley," Po said gently.

Small tears ran down Halley's cheeks, and she looked away, embarrassed.

"Do you really think Adele was involved, Halley? Maybe it's your deep sadness in losing a friend and wanting some resolution to that."

Halley looked back at Po. She dabbed at her eyes with a napkin, then shrugged her narrow shoulders. "Somebody killed Ollie, Po," was all she answered.

Po reached across the table and covered Halley's hand with her own. "Yes, someone did that terrible thing, Halley. And someone will pay for it—and hopefully that will be soon."

But much later that night, Po stood in her robe on the back deck, looking up at the same sky that Ollie Harrington loved with such passion. She thought back on her conversation with Halley Peterson and wondered about her own hollow words. Halley was lashing out at Adele, she thought, because there was no one else to focus on. She was the visible sign of the loss Halley had suffered in losing her friend. But killing her own brother?

Po shuddered. A breeze whipped her robe about her legs and she stepped back inside, closing the French doors behind her. It was so unsettling: Her conversation with Halley, and even more than that, the uncomfortable feeling that there were secrets at 210 Kingfish Drive that threatened people she knew. There was a feeling of dread building up in the neighborhood—the place where she'd raised her children, walked alone at night, and left her doors unlocked. Having that lifestyle threatened was disturbing, unsettling, and in the end, made Po angry. She walked to the stove and put a kettle on to brew some tea before bed. It would be hard to sleep, she knew. It was time to do something.

CHAPTER 13

Joe Bates shuffled around the side of the wide garage and walked silently toward the pond in the back of the big house. The sun was slowly climbing up above the trees in the east and Joe could feel the soft glow on his leathered skin. *It'll be a warm day,* he suspected. A late fall day tinged with impending winter. He clutched the thermos of coffee and planted one foot after another, drinking in the morning air. Not that the days had all been so great lately, but early morning seemed another world, another time, and he could forget for awhile the things that had gone bad, the dark days and dangers all around him.

It was still quiet at this hour, before the jostling groups of foul-mouthed workers invaded his home. They'd come today, even on a Saturday, he knew. No peace. But for this brief hour, it was just Joe and his pond and the soft flat lilies floating along the surface. But no Ollie, who used to bring him blueberry muffins that he'd make all by himself, and they'd sit beside the pond while the last remnants of the sky's galaxies faded into the light of day. And he'd let Ollie go on and on and on about those planets and stars that were so real to him they nearly became family. Lordy, how Joe missed that boy. Loved Ollie like a son, quirks and all. He was a good boy. Not sharp-tongued like that sister of his. Not cruel like his father. Kind and gentle, just like his sweet mother, God bless her soul.

The thought of Oliver gripped Joe fiercely, and he paused on the flagstone pathway, his head cloudy and sad. Then, with the commitment he'd made to Ollie, he continued on toward his pond, trying to push the painful thoughts aside. Old Missus Harrington had left it up to him to watch over Ollie—even gave him the apartment up behind the garage so he'd stay close. And what'd he done? Let him get killed. And now he'd have to do something about it. Bring honor back to the boy. And now at last he knew how to do it. He'd right the wrong. Just like the Bible told him to do.

Joe settled down on one of the boulders that ringed the lily pond. He remembered when they lifted those rocks in place years and years ago. Brought in a huge old crane and dropped them right in place. Directed it hisself. Joe carefully unscrewed the top of his thermos and felt the steam rise up his nose, wetting the thin hairs.

He hadn't understood Oliver's ranting at first. Ollie'd been so mad, he didn't make much sense. The boy didn't get mad much, but this time he thought he'd lost not just what was his, but a part of his soul, he told Joe. People given him the short end of things all his life, he'd said. But this time it was wrong. They couldn't take it away from him. He wouldn't let it happen.

Joe hadn't quite understood, thought Ollie was talking off the top of his head like he sometimes did. But now Joe finally understood. And finally he had the proof he needed to make it right. He'd show the high and mighty Adele Harrington, sure as he knew his name was Joe Bates.

Joe leaned forward, staring into the water, cleaned by the dozens of Koi that swam in slow circles just beneath the surface. Soon his boy would rest in peace. Joe bowed his head and briefly removed the faded Royals baseball cap from his head. With gnarled fingers, he made a sign of the cross over his chest. *Requiescat in pace*. Least he could do. He squeezed his eyes shut and wrapped his arms around his body, silently praying he'd have the strength to do this one last thing for Ollie. He slipped the cap back over his thinning white hair.

With his eyes closed, Joe didn't see the shadow fall across the pond. And with his hearing not so perfect anymore, he missed the light play of tennis shoes across the path, missed the lifting of the large stone rock behind his back, up in the air over his head. Felt only the rush of air as the large rock crushed down unforgiving on the top of his head.

For a brief second, Joe saw the lilies and the fish look up at him. Spread apart. Welcome him.

And then all was black, and Joe's body folded over and rolled off the rock as gracefully as a seal that was through sunning himself, and slipped silently beneath the cool, soothing water of his pond.

Requiescat in pace.

CHAPTER 14

Maggie's new van was parked at the curb, directly in front of Selma's store. She stood on the sidewalk beside it, beaming. "Okay, ladies," she said, "this may be your only chance to ride in my new chariot before it's full of dog hair and tools."

"Mags, it's beautiful," Kate said, admiring the shiny white van with "Helmers Pet Care" painted along the side in bright blue swirling letters.

"Thanks, Kate." Maggie put her hands on her hips, her eyes bright. "I'm keeping the truck for old times' sake—

but isn't this a hunk? And before I take out a row for cages, it will nicely fit all eight of us, I do believe." She slid open the big side door to reveal three rows of seats.

"Very nice, Maggie," Po said. "It's about time you got something for yourself. And it's a vast improvement from that rusty truck, beloved or not."

"Let's get this show on the road," Selma said. "I want to be back before the Saturday crowd comes in and drives my staff crazy."

"Selma, don't fret so," Susan said, "things will be fine. You need to start taking some time off, away from the store."

"And realize that it really will survive without you," Leah chimed in.

Selma waved off their words and pulled herself up into the van, puffing a little as she settled herself near the window. "Hand me my bag, will you?" she asked Phoebe, who promptly spun her diminutive body up next to Selma, her own backpack and Selma's sewing bag in tow.

"Very cool, Maggie," Phoebe said as she reached down and helped Eleanor up into the van.

Kate, Leah, and Susan slipped around the settled bodies into the wide back seat, Po joined Maggie in the front, and in minutes the Queen Bees were off, heading down Elderberry Road toward the Harrington mansion.

"Why do you suppose Adele wanted us all to come?" Maggie called back over her shoulder. "You'd think looking at quilts on the beds would be the last thing she'd be thinking about."

Po shifted on the seat. "I think she's just wanting some

assurance that something in her planning is going right and is under her control. She seemed jittery yesterday when I talked to her."

"Very jittery," Kate piped up from the back of the van. "And a little paranoid. She stopped me yesterday as I was biking by the house—she was pulling out of the drive in that long Cadillac of hers—and wanted to know if I had seen anyone suspicious in the neighborhood. I almost felt sorry for her."

"This is an enormous undertaking for her," Po said. "Max said it's costing more than she had thought, as things do."

"Well, maybe we can cheer her up a bit," Leah said. "I think our quilt tops are beautiful."

"Of course they are!" Phoebe said.

"And we're here," Maggie announced, pulling into the driveway.

"This is the first time in weeks I've been able to see all the way back to the carriage house," Po said as Maggie pulled over to the side of the drive and turned off the ignition. "Not a truck in sight."

"But there will be," Selma said. "The renovation crew is here seven days a week, old Mrs. Porter tells me. She said she can hear the commotion all the way from her house on the corner. She's ready to spit fire at Adele. Her husband patrols the street, just waiting for something to go wrong."

"A truck ran over the Porter's new chrysanthemum bed, Mrs. P announced last week in the supermarket," Eleanor added. "Unhappy neighbors are not a good thing."

"But it is a good thing we beat the mob. Shall we get this over with?" Po asked, opening the van door and stepping out into the drive.

The others followed suit, and when they walked up the wide fan of steps leading to the front door, Adele was waiting for them.

"You are prompt, as always," Adele said, holding open the door. "Thank you for coming."

"Like I haven't been dying to see the inside of this place?" Phoebe answered. She touched Adele on the arm and smiled brightly. "This is amazing, Adele. I want to see every single inch of it."

Po watched the exchange and noticed the instinctive tightening of Adele's muscles at Phoebe's light touch. The poor woman probably isn't touched much, she thought, and the thought made Po suddenly sad.

"I thought we would go directly up to the guest rooms and lay each quilt out on a bed so I can get a feeling for how they fit in," Adele said, and led the group of women carrying their quilt tops up a wide, winding staircase to the second floor. Her back was rod straight, and her face unreadable as she walked next to Po.

"Maybe my sweet Emma will get married here," Phoebe whispered to Kate, her small hand sliding along the walnut banister.

"Phoebe, she's three years old." Kate laughed.

"Well, one needs to plan." Phoebe lifted her chin up into the air.

When they reached the top, Adele waved the Bees into

separate rooms, directing them to smooth their tops out on the beds.

Po walked into the small room that had been Oliver's. Everything was the same as the last time she had seen it—the book case filled with books, the small desk positioned beneath the window with a yellow pad of paper and cup of pencils ready for his use, the copy of Professor Fellers' book. She stretched out her quilt on the narrow bed and stood back.

"It's perfect," Adele said from the doorway. She looked at the stars shining up from the bed.

Po turned. "You think Ollie would have approved?"

Adele nodded. A sad smile eased the sternness in her face.

"This must be difficult for you," Po said.

"I don't let things be difficult, Po. It's a choice."

"Not always, Adele. But you do seem to handle things that would get the better of most of us."

Adele didn't answer. She walked over to the window and stood next to Oliver's telescope, pointed up to the sky.

Po walked over to her side.

"I didn't neglect my brother, you know." Adele's voice was so soft Po could barely hear her words. "I did the best I could under the circumstances. Things are not always as they seem."

Po felt an urge to wrap an arm around Adele, to pull her close and comfort her. But she knew instinctively the slight openness Adele had allowed would disappear in a heartbeat if she disrupted the moment.

Adele looked back at the quilt, and when she spoke

this time, the softness was gone, and the protective shield was back in place. "The colors are good and the paint color goes well with it, don't you think?"

Po nodded. She looked around the room and agreed that the deep blue of the walls and the white smooth woodwork were perfect for the multi-starred quilt. And then her gaze settled on Ollie's desk and the yellow pad, waiting to be used. "Ollie didn't use a computer, did he? But he loved to write. I can't imagine writing anything in long-hand anymore."

"He wrote all the time, even as a child. It was one thing he could do well, even when he didn't always communicate well in conversation. Some people are like that, you know.

"He wanted to write a book someday. That Peterson girl wanted all his writings, but I wouldn't give them to her. Why would I do that?" Adele shook her head and bent over to smooth the quilt with the flat of her hand. "Everyone wants a piece of Ollie," she said softly.

"People liked your brother, Adele," Po said.

Adele didn't answer, but the slight nod of her head and sad smile told Po that she knew it to be true.

"Here you two are," Selma said, walking into the room. "I think all the quilts are going to work beautifully, Adele." Adele turned around. "You've all done a nice job. Once they're completely finished, we'll have an open house so everyone can see. And now we will have coffee and scones down on the back veranda before you leave."

"No need for that," Selma began, but Adele had already walked out into the hallway and started down the steps, motioning for everyone to gather their quilt tops and follow her.

"I guess we'll have coffee and scones," Selma said to Po, shrugging her shoulders. "But let's keep it short, Po. I have a full day ahead of me."

"We all do, Selma. I agree. Short it will be."

The wrought iron table on the brick veranda was set with an embroidered tablecloth, and a platter of blueberry scones sat in the center, next to a vase of bright yellow mums and pot of sweet butter. Adele urged them to make themselves comfortable and slipped back inside to get the coffee.

"This is so lovely," Po said, admiring the fairytale setting. She stood next to Kate at the stone railing of the wide veranda and looked over the yard. Sunlight streamed through the trees, casting soft shadows across the recently mowed grass.

"This backyard is awesome," Phoebe said, walking up beside them. "So cool! If we put in a slide and wading pool, it would be a perfect park for Emma and Jude."

"It doesn't have a wading pool, Phoebe, but there's a pond down beyond that clump of trees," Kate said, pointing to the flagstone path that led to Joe's pond. "Joe Bates—the gardener—tends to it so lovingly you'd think Monet was going to show up to paint lilies any day,"

"I want to see it," Phoebe said. She looked back toward the French doors. "Let's go look. Adele is still inside."

"I'm sure she'd be happy for us to admire the grounds," Po said. "She's put so much effort into cleaning everything up." The three women walked down the steps leading into the backyard and walked slowly toward the pond, admiring the touch of color in the tips of the Japanese Maples. "I came out here a few times with Oliver and Joe Bates to see the pond—it was lovely then, but now the yard is so green and lush you want to roll on it."

"This will be a magical place next spring when all the hydrangeas and dogwoods bloom," Kate said. "I think you're right about it being an ideal spot for a wedding."

"Maybe you and P.J. can tie the knot here," Phoebe said.

Kate laughed. "Do you know something I don't, Phoebe?"

Po listened to the banter, wondering if Phoebe's prediction would come true any time soon. Things seemed to be heading in that direction, and having Kate and P.J. married would certainly fill her with joy. She thought of her dear friend Liz, and knew Kate's mother must be watching over this relationship with a bit of joy herself.

"This is wonderful," Phoebe said, walking around a shade grove of hydrangeas circling a clump of towering pine trees. "A pond in the park."

"Looks like Joe beat us out here," Kate said as they neared the pond. She pointed to a thermos lying by the rocks.

"I wonder if he's around," Po said. "I don't want to frighten him. His hearing isn't very good anymore." She looked over toward the gardens as Phoebe and Kate rounded the mound of rocks on one side of the pond.

"Po," Kate said, staring into the pond. "Po, come here." Her voice was urgent.

Phoebe followed the point of Kate's finger down toward the edge of the pond where a clump of lilies fanned out, separating from one another. A faded blue KC Royals cap floated between the leaves.

Po stared down into the water. And as the lilies moved in the chilly breeze, she spotted what caused the urgency in Kate's voice. The blue ball cap moved slowly away, and beneath it, a school of brilliantly colored koi swam in and out of the waving strands of Joe Bates' thinning white hair.

CHAPTER 15

Going to Marla's bakery and café Sunday morning with Leah Sarandon was a tradition as old as Po and Leah's friendship, and it was in keeping with that tradition and nothing else that found the two women sitting in the busy bakery the day after finding Joe Bates' body. They were surrounded by gossip thicker than the syrup Marla served with her blueberry pancakes.

"Everyone and his brother will be in here this morning," Po said, looking around at the nearly full breakfast spot. The line was beginning to form outside the windows and would soon be winding down Elderberry Road, people coming from church or home or a college dorm, enjoying the crisp fall day.

"Bad news seems to bring out everyone," Leah said. "I guess they just want answers. But gossip is such a bad place to look for them." She sat back as a young waitress put a platter of eggs down in front of her.

"It's so ugly. All this mess," Po said, the experience of finding Joe's body still tightly wrapped around her heart. Adele had spotted them out at the pond, staring at the grisly sight. She'd rushed across the lawn, her face a portrait of horror and shame.

Phoebe and Kate helped Adele back to the house, while Po called the ambulance and police from her cell phone. She had stayed there at the lily pond, feeling an instinctive need to guard Joe until help came. Within minutes the driveway was once again filled with spinning blue lights and the kind of attention no new business would wish upon itself. After all the Bees were questioned by the police, Po and Kate stayed on with Adele for a short time, urging her to rest and wondering if they could help contact any of Joe's relatives. But there were no relatives, Adele said, that much she knew about the old man. And then she had collected herself, looked out at the garage and carriage house, and announced that she'd now need to do some renovating of the apartment above the garage. It could be a suite—perhaps for honeymooners, she'd remarked. Po had cringed, but was grateful no policeman was around at the time. Sometimes Adele was her own worst enemy.

"Ladies, I thought you'd never get here." Marla Patrick, her brow dotted with perspiration, sided up to the small table near the window. She wiped her thick hands on a smudged apron and leaned over Po and Leah. "Who would have imagined that skinny woman had it in her?"

"What are you talking about, Marla," Po asked, though the answer was only too clear. Marla had already convicted Adele Harrington. And that meant there were many othersin the room sharing the same sentiment. Marla's opinions were usually fueled by others.

"Adele Harrington, that's who. Drowned old Joe as sure as I'm breathing. I knew she was up to no good soon as she came back to this town." Marla straightened up and scanned the room to make sure her waitresses were being attentive to customers' needs. Then she hunkered low again, speaking in a whisper. "Tom Adler's over there with his wife—" Marla nodded toward the other side of the room. "Comes in right after Mass at Saint Boniface's. Said that he was over at the house the other day and heard Adele say she wanted to get rid of old Joe."

"Tom isn't too fond of Adele, Marla," Po said, trying to soften the statement that she herself had heard come out of Adele's mouth.

"Tom hates her, sure. Would love the place to fail, and then he'd scoop it up himself. But that doesn't matter a whit. What matters is that the Harrington woman will stop at nothing to make things go her way."

"Marla, you don't know that," Leah said, feeling the need to protect Adele Harrington from the surging wave of gossip.

"I know what I know," Marla said, her small green eyes moving from one woman to the next. "I don't like to speak ill of anyone, you know that, but we need this evil to stop so we can get back to normal here in Crestwood. We need all those out-of-town folks to keep coming to Elderberry Road. Our businesses need those folks, Po, and they'll stop coming if this evil cloud hangs around much longer. You know that and I know that. Adele Harrington needs to be put in jail or driven out of town."

Driven out of town. The words lingered in Po's head as she looked over at Tom Adler. He was standing now, handing his wife her sweater and collecting his bill. He would certainly like the B&B to fail, she thought. His development business had come on hard times recently, and developing the Harrington estate would help it considerably, everyone knew that. Po watched him talking with his wife and greeting the mayor, who had just come in the door. Could Tom possibly have done something as awful as drown poor Joe Bates to make Adele look bad? But if not Tom, who? Marla was right about one thing—the activities at 210 Kingfish Drive needed to stop now—before any more damage was done.

"Po, a penny for your thoughts," Leah said. "Marla has moved on, you can come out of your cocoon."

Po smiled. "Sorry, Leah. I was lost in thought. None of this is making any sense." She picked up her coffee cup and drank slowly, nodding to a neighbor vacating the table next to them.

"Adele may not be the most lovable person in town,"

Leah said, "but I think Marla is wrong about her. Besides, you don't kill someone just to get them off your property."

"No, I would hope not." Po fingered her napkin, thinking about Adele. She knew in her heart that Leah was right. But things were certainly not looking good for Adele.

"Po?"

Po looked up into the sad eyes of Halley Peterson, standing beside the table next to them.

"Oh, Halley," Po said, reaching out to touch the offered hand off the librarian. "I am so sorry about Joe."

Halley nodded, forcing a smile to her lips, and Po noticed moisture gathering in her eyes.

"It's so awful, Po," Halley said.

Jed Fellers walked up behind Halley and nodded at Po and Leah. His face was drawn, his eyes troubled. "Hi Po. Leah. Not the best of days, is it?"

"Hi, Jed," Po said. "No, it's most definitely not. It's kind of amazing how quickly news spreads in Crestwood."

"Halley heard it on the news early this morning," Jed said. "I think it's all over town."

"I couldn't stay in my apartment," Halley said. "I wanted to scream or beat on someone or be sick. When I called Jed, he suggested a walk instead."

"Halley was probably one of the few people in Joe's life since Ollie's death," Jed said.

"In these weeks since Ollie's death," Halley said, "Joe and I spent time together, going through the few writings and things of Ollie's that Joe was able to wrest from Adele. He was such a good man, and he certainly didn't deserve to have his life end like this."

"No one deserves something like this, Halley," Po said. She watched Jed order tea and scones for Halley, grateful that the sweet woman had someone to lean on during these difficult times. She was still dealing with Ollie's death, and now to have another tragedy touch her life must be nearly unbearable.

"Jed has been good to let me lean on him," Halley said, as if reading Po's mind. She looked over at him and smiled.

Po watched the exchange. A slight blush colored Halley's cheeks when she looked at Jed, and his returning smile was comforting. She wondered if a romance might be in the making between the two. They were an unlikely couple, but the difference in age seemed to fall away in the looks they exchanged. And Jed was certainly a very young fifty. Something lovely in the middle of all this sordidness would be a good thing for everyone, she thought.

"Do you know if there will be a service for Joe?" Halley asked. "I wanted to call Adele, but she doesn't like me very much, and I doubt if she'd give me the time of day."

"I'll try to find out, Halley, and I'll let you know," Po said.

"Halley and I would be happy to pack up Joe's things," Jed said. "Adele probably doesn't want to be bothered with it. She didn't like Joe much either, as I understand it."

"No, she didn't," Po said. But she also didn't like strangers on her property, and Po doubted if Jed's kind offer would be received well. It was a shame, because Halley cared about the man and would treat his belongings with respect. Adele would most likely shovel everything into a dumpster.

Leah finished the last trace of her eggs and sat back, her

napkin beside her plate. "On a happier note, congratulations, Jed. I hear the book served its purpose."

Jed laughed. "I guess you could say that."

Leah looked over at Po. "Jed has been offered the department chair. A perk for being published."

"Good for you, Jed. You certainly deserve it," Po said. She remembered those tense days when Sam was a young professor, needing that affirmation from the college administration. Well, this was good. And they needed good news these days. Jed accepted the compliment, but seemed uncomfortable with the attention and soon had turned the conversation back to Po and the quilters, wondering if they had finished their quilts for 210 Kingfish Drive.

"Almost," Po said. "We're finishing borders and backs now, and then they will all be quilted by a wonderful lady over in Parkville, Missouri. It's been a nice project for all of us, except for all the grisly goings on over at the Harrington place."

Po reached for the check that the waitress placed beside her empty plate. She placed a bill down on top of it and pushed out her chair while Leah followed. "You two enjoy your breakfast," she said.

The two women picked up their bags and wove their way through the narrow space between tables to the front door. "Let's make a getaway before Marla heaps more gossip on our shoulders," Leah said softly into Po's ear. "She means well, but sometimes Marla talks entirely too much."

Po agreed. She liked Marla, but her small bakery was becoming a hotbed of gossip, and sometimes that did more harm than good. The town needed concrete answers to make this unrest go away, not a sea of suspicion and innuendo. Leah pushed open the door, and Po followed her out into the bright cool sunshine of the fall day. And then the two women stopped, stepping back instinctively into the shadow of Marla's awning.

Tom Adler stood across the street next to a pear tree, staring through the closed car window of Adele Harrington's empty Cadillac. His head lifted, and he scanned the block, looking for something, someone. As Po and Leah watched, a figure emerged from Max Elliot's law office a few doors down. Adele Harrington was dressed in a bright blue silk suit. A leather portfolio hung from her shoulder, and she walked down the short stand of steps and headed quickly toward her car. Sunday walkers passed her by, some greeting her, others casting her curious, suspicious looks, but Adele ignored them all, her eyes cast straight ahead.

Po and Leah watched Tom step back behind the clump of trees, hidden from Adele's sight until she reached the car and removed her keys from her purse. For a minute Po thought Tom was going to say something or do something harmful to Adele. But then she saw his wife wave to him from a bright red BMW parked a few spaces back, and Tom lowered his head and hurried to his car.

CHAPTER 16

Po and Leah watched the long car taking the corner fast enough to scatter leaves in all directions.

"What do you suppose that's about?" Leah asked.

"I don't know, but I'm glad Tom's wife had the good sense to remind him that she was waiting in the car."

"Did Adele see him, do you think?" Po shifted her purse on her shoulder, and she and Leah began walking down the street toward Gus Schuette's bookstore. "And I wonder what she was doing at Max's office on a Sunday morning?"

"With all that's going on at her home, she may have needed some legal advice."

Po had had the same thought, and dear Max would meet someone in need in the middle of the night if they asked. She glanced over at the small brick building that housed his office and noticed his car was gone. He'd clearly come in just to solve Adele's problem, whatever that might have been. She'd see him later that day—Max hadn't missed a Sunday dinner at the Paltrow home in nearly a year—and she wondered if he'd bring this up. Probably not. Max was a paradigm of discretion, one of the many things Po was coming to appreciate—and to love—about him.

Leah and Po reached Gus's bookstore and walked into the shadowy haven. Gus had modeled the store after an old bookstore he visited in London—hardwood floors, paintings placed on available wall space, and lots of small rooms crammed with shelves and library ladders and over-stuffed chairs begging to be used. Po loved it here, and the owner, too. Gus and his wife Rita had been in her life longer than she could remember. Sam used to tell Gus that he and Po had single handedly paid for the Schuette kids' education with the money spent in the store.

Today Gus sat on a chair behind the wooden checkout counter, his head lowered over a book, his glasses hovering low on a wide, misshapen nose. He looked up and stood as the entrance bell pinged. His face broke into a grin. "My Sunday ladies are here at last. Let the day begin." He set his book on the counter and automatically reached beneath the counter for two reserved copies of the Sunday *New York Times.* "I could set my clock by you two," he said, handing them the thick newspapers.

"You say that every single Sunday, Gus," Po said.

Gus laughed. "What would we do without our rituals, Po?"

Po smiled. The familiarity of routines and dear people were what Crestwood was all about. Perhaps that was true of small towns everywhere. But this Sunday morning routine was one of her favorites. She and Leah had started it years ago, when Leah was a brand new professor at Canterbury College. Sam Paltrow soon discovered his new employee's husband loved Sunday morning golf as much as he did. So while Sam and Tim swung clubs, Po and Leah, the sixteen years between them melting away in a flash of an eye, began their Sunday morning walks to Elderberry Road for Marla's eggs or waffles, for talk and friendship, and always, for a quick trip to Gus's store for the Sunday *Times*.

"Kate was in soon as the doors opened." Gus looked over his shoulder and nodded toward a side reading room. "She and P.J. are in the back, sitting on the floor with a stack of books in front of them, just like when they were kids."

"Except he isn't pulling her ponytail like he used to."

Gus laughed and at that moment P.J. and Kate walked into the room, their arms loaded with books. They were dressed in jeans and turtlenecks, windbreakers wrapped around their waists, their faces flushed. Po suspected they had been riding bikes along the river, leaving the town's worries behind for a while.

"We supported Gus's kids' education," Po said. "Looks like you two are supporting his retirement."

"As it should be." Gus grinned at Kate. "Lord knows you gave me enough trouble when you were a kid. Always reading. Never buying. Glad to see things have changed."

Kate punched his arm lightly. "You're all talk, Gus Schuette. You loved our trouble, and you know it." She turned toward Po and Leah. "So Po, what's the word at Marla's?" Kate's face grew serious with the question, knowing the café would have been rife with talk of Joe Bates' death.

Po watched P.J. loop an arm over Kate's shoulder and draw her to his side. She knew exactly what he was thinking. Kate, murder is dangerous business.

"As you might guess, Adele is getting the brunt of the speculation."

"It doesn't look very good for her," P.J. said. "Too many people heard her talking about Joe, criticizing him, wanting him off her property. But I don't think there's anything but anecdotal evidence at this point."

"Don't know why anybody'd want to murder that old man," Gus said.

"Did you know him, Gus?" Leah asked. "Joe was such a recluse, most people only knew him by reputation."

"Except for people our age," Po said. "In his youth, Joe was the person we all went to when grass wouldn't grow or we needed the best ground cover or our dogwoods weren't blooming. I don't think there's a home in my neighborhood that hasn't been touched by Joe Bates."

"He was smitten with Mrs. Harrington, I think," Gus said. "Absolutely devoted to her."

"You're right, Gus. And after awhile, he only worked for her, then moved in and that's when we didn't see much of him anymore," Po added.

Gus rang up Kate's books and handed her the receipt. "I was surprised when Joe came in here recently. Almost didn't recognize the fellow, been so long since I'd seen him."

"Joe was here?" Po asked.

"Just a few days ago. Wanted me to order him a book. He wasn't wanting to talk, though I told him how good it was to see him and tried to chitchat a bit. Showed him some new garden books. I watched him through the window when he left and saw him trudging back toward 210 Kingfish Drive, head down, face a mask of sadness. He seemed determined, kind of, like he was on a mission, but you could see that Ollie's death had taken a toll on him."

"Maybe he was finally trying to move beyond the Harrington House—to begin a life without Ollie."

"Maybe." Gus scratched his square chin. "Maybe so. He was, well, agitated. But I hadn't seen him for so long, that could have been his normal look."

Po frowned. "Joe was a good sort. His murder is so troubling and senseless. It's awful for the whole town, but above all, for Adele Harrington. Having someone murdered in her backyard isn't going to help promote her bed and breakfast any."

"Some folks say it might have been an accident. Adele has quite a temper. Maybe she just meant to shake him up," Gus offered.

"I'm afraid there'll be a lot of 'maybes' floating around,"

Kate said. "And they will only hurt Adele." She turned toward P.J. "Does all this speculation hurt the case, P.J.?"

P.J. shrugged. "Probably not. The investigation will go forward on its own course. But what speculation does is hurt innocent people."

Kate nodded. "I don't know what it is about Adele Harrington—she's insulted so many people—but there's more to her than that. When Phoebe and I helped her into the house yesterday after those awful moments at the lily pond, we could see agony in her eyes. Real, genuine hurt. She mumbled something we couldn't quite understand, something about her mother. And Ollie. And how horrible this would have been for them both."

"I've seen traces of that, too, Kate. Something real and decent," Po said.

"Well, it wouldn't hurt the woman to let a few others see that side of her," Gus said. "Rita and I invited her to a book signing here at the store—one of those cocktail things we do. We thought maybe she'd like getting to know some folks—"

"And maybe fill her B&B library from books she'd buy here?" Leah teased.

"Sure, a little business. A little pleasure. But you know my Rita, she decided this is what a newcomer in town needed and she would have introduced her to everyone within fifty miles."

"But she turned you down," Kate said.

"Flatter than Kansas," Gus said. "And was rude in the process."

"It's a protection, I think," Po said. "But I think in time she'll warm up."

"Well, let's hope she's not finding herself warming up in the cooler."

Po shook her head. "You're hopeless, Gus, and on that note, I need to get moving. Leah and I are going to stop by Adele's to see if there's anything we can do."

But when Po and Leah drove down Kingfish Drive a few minutes later, they could see that the iron gates leading to the drive were closed and locked, and in the distance, crowding the curve of the drive, three police cars stood guard over a murder scene.

That night, Po's Sunday dinner group started out small. The tradition her Sam had started years ago still held the unknown—twenty people might show up—or four—one never knew. But no matter the number, those who came were welcome and could always count on a tasty meal that Po seemed to whip up out of nothing. Dinner, martinis, and always dessert. It was a mystery how it all came about, but one her friends and neighbors were eternally grateful for. This Sunday night, Maggie, Max, P.J. and Kate, Leah, her husband Tim, and Eleanor dropped in, each carrying a bottle of wine or loaf of bread—and tidbits about Adele Harrington. Po had tried to reach Halley, thinking she might enjoy the gathering, but she had to leave a message when Halley didn't answer.

P.J. manned the grill while Kate prepared drinks, and Po urged everyone out to the deck to enjoy the wonderful starry evening, and maybe the last outdoor gathering before winter set in. They'd gotten a later-than-usual start and P.J. was piling shrimp and vegetables on the grill.

"I got a strange call this morning," Maggie said, standing near the deck railing. She wore faded jeans and a soft fleece jacket. "Adele Harrington called me at home. She asked me to open the clinic so she could bring Emerson in to board him." Maggie eyed the platter of Thai spring rolls that Eleanor was placing on the long deck table. "Isn't that kind of odd? Emerson seems to be her one true friend—you'd think she would want to keep him close, especially at times like this."

Eleanor pushed up the sleeves of her silky red blouse and handed Maggie a paper plate with a spoonful of peanut sauce for the spring rolls, which were overflowing with tiny pink shrimp and flecks of cilantro and mint. "That's odd," Eleanor said. "Adele loves that dog more than life itself. I ran into her down at the river park the other day while my yoga class was exercising on the lawn. She looked like she hadn't slept in a few days, but every time Emerson rubbed against her, her face relaxed and she seemed almost happy."

"Seems like Adele placed more than one call this morning." Leah looked over at Max. "Po and I saw her leaving your office bright and early."

Max took a chilled martini from the tray Kate held in front of him. "This is a difficult time for her," he said. "She wanted to check some insurance policies to make sure the property was covered. She just needed assurance that her legal affairs were in order."

"That sounds ominous," Maggie said. "Isn't that something you do before you die—or go off to jail?"

Po listened to the conversation as she walked back and forth between the kitchen and the deck, piling napkins and silverware on the table, bringing out pitchers of water and salt and pepper. The night was so pleasant and the group so small that she'd decided they would settle into the comfortable deck chairs and settees and eat right there beneath the stars. She had thought about calling Adele to see if she needed company and would like to join them, but she knew as surely as anything that she'd be turned down. And with good reason. Were she in Adele's situation right now, socializing would be the last thing on her mind.

"Did Adele talk about Joe's funeral at all?" P.J. asked from his position at the grill. "They won't release the body for a couple days, but someone should be making plans to give the guy a decent burial."

"No. I asked, but she ignored me," Max said. "I don't think she feels responsible for burying Joe, and I suppose, officially, she isn't."

"Reverend Gottrey will take care of it if no one steps up to the plate," Po said. "I called him about it today. It's so sad when there's no family—or even close friends—to take care of these things."

P.J. carried a platter of skewers stacked with plump, spicy grilled shrimp and scallops to the table. Po followed with orzo sprinkled with feta cheese and snow peas, a basket of sour dough rolls, and a heaping bowl of spinach salad. She slipped her arms through a thick blue cardigan sweater, fixed herself a plate, and settled onto the glider beside Max. "It's good to be with friends," she said softly.

Beside her, Max nodded. He reached out and touched her hand, then looked up at the stars flung wide across the black sky. "This sky makes me think of Ollie. He was so brilliant when it came to the heavens."

"I never even met him, and that's so odd in a small town like this," Maggie said.

"I think you had to fit into a certain compartment of his life," Leah said. "Otherwise your paths wouldn't cross. His life seemed to be the college, his classes with Jed, the library, and his home. Being there with Joe."

"And Halley Peterson," Po added. "It's somehow comforting to know that Ollie had a friend like Halley. And it's clear to me she genuinely cared for him. And for Joe, too. The past couple weeks have been difficult for her."

"P.J. and I saw her today after we left Gus's store." Kate rose and put her empty plate on the table, then propped herself up on the wide railing, her arms folded over a thick cotton sweater Po had knitted for her. "She and Jed were walking toward campus, deep in conversation. I don't think they even saw us. Halley looked upset, and so sad. And Jed was clearly a comforting shoulder to lean on."

"Jed was so good to Ollie," Leah said. "They have that in common. I'm glad Halley has someone to talk with. As busy as Jed is, he's making time for her, and that's a good thing."

"Coffee anyone?" Po asked, rising from the glider.

"And I brought ice cream," Eleanor added. "Let me help, Po."

As the two women headed for the French doors leading inside, the sound of a siren in the distance cut through the crisp night air. Eleanor paused at the door. "Such a mournful sound," she said. "And it always means distressing news for someone."

Po looked out into the darkness. Tiny lights illuminated the giant oaks and pine trees in her backyard—a perfect, peaceful setting. But she felt it, too, the unsettling feeling of unknown lives being changed in an instant by an auto crash, a heart attack, a random, freak accident. She walked on into the house. "Let's hope it's no one we know, El."

Eleanor busied herself in the kitchen, scooping large portions of ice cream in bowls while Po filled a tray with cups, cream and sugar, and the coffee pot. "Fudge sauce?" Po asked.

But before she could open the refrigerator, a different sound, much closer, joined the sirens.

"Now that's a sound you don't often hear," Eleanor said, wiping her hands on a towel and glancing toward Po's front hall. "It's your doorbell. Who in heaven's name uses your doorbell, Po?"

"Not many people," Po admitted. "Not when they know it's just as easy to push it open and walk in." Po walked quickly toward the front of her house. The sound of the sirens quickened her step as she reached the front door and pulled it open.

Po looked out into the darkness, and before she could speak, Halley Peterson flung herself into Po's arms.

CHAPTER 17

"Oh, Halley, dear," Po murmured, drawing the disheveled woman into the front hall. Halley's brown hair was loose, falling over her shoulders. A sweater was wrapped carelessly around her shoulders and her Canterbury tee shirt was half-tucked into the waist of her jeans. For a brief moment, Po thought she might have been in an accident. "Are you all right?"

Halley drew apart, wiping away the tears that streamed down her cheeks with the back of her hand. She nodded, her throat too tight for words to pass.

"Come in," Po said, and drew Halley through the entryway and into the warm glow of the family room lights. Eleanor brought a glass of water over to her while Po urged Halley to sit on the couch. In the distance, the sirens increased in volume, filling the night air with a strident symphony.

Kate rushed in from the back deck, her dark hair flying. "Po," she called out, "there's a fire somewhere. We can smell the smoke." She stopped suddenly, spotting Halley.

"It's Joe—" Halley said, looking up at Kate.

"Joe?" Po asked gently. The wild look in Halley's eyes was disturbing. And now her words weren't making sense.

Halley shook her head, as if trying to straighten her thoughts, to put them in order. "Joe's apartment," Halley said. Her voice was almost a whisper. "The Harrington's garage is on fire."

By then the rest of the Sunday supper crowd had come inside and were busying themselves in the kitchen, putting dishes in the dishwasher, talking softly, and hoping Halley could provide more information as they listened to the soft voices across the room.

"Halley, were you there?" Po said, sitting beside the distraught woman.

Halley nodded. "I went over to see if Adele would let me in Joe's place—to get...to get some things. The police were gone by then, and I knew Adele wouldn't wait long to throw everything out of Joe's apartment. I wanted to salvage some things Ollie had given Joe, some things that meant a lot to Ollie and Joe. She almost threw me off the property, threatened to call the police back. Said she'd had enough bad things happen to her."

Po handed Halley a tissue, and she continued.

"So I went back tonight, determined to not let all remnants of those two good men end in a dumpster." A sad smile eased the tense lines outlining her face. "I knew where Joe kept a key to his place, and I decided I'd just go in and take some things. I know it's wrong, but I didn't care. I walked along the bushes hidden from the house, and was half-way there when I spotted the flames."

"And then?"

"And then I was so frightened that I turned and ran in the opposite direction toward the street—I didn't want Adele to see me. And then I..." Halley paused and seemed to be deciding what to say next. When she spoke again, her words were planned, thoughtful, careful. "Then I wandered around the neighborhood for awhile, away from the Harrington house but close enough to hear the sirens, not knowing where to go. I saw your lights, Po. And you've been so kind to me—"

A knock on the back door broke into the quiet room.

Max walked over to it and pushed it open for Jed Fellers, his face washed in worry. "Halley? Is she here?"

Max nodded and motioned for Jed to come in. "She's in need of friends, I think," he said softly and motioned toward the living area.

Jed smiled his thanks and walked over to the couch. He looked at Halley's tear-stained face. "Are you okay, Halley? I was so worried when I got your message. I could hear those sirens all the way over on campus—but couldn't find you."

Halley wiped the tears from her cheek and looked up at Jed. "Jed, it was so awful. I know you told me not to go over there, that Adele would turn me away. But I had to—"

Po got up to make room for Jed on the couch. "Sit, Jed," she said, and walked over to Max while Halley repeated the story to a distraught Jed.

"Po," Max whispered, "P.J. and I are going to run over and check on Adele. We'll be back shortly."

Po nodded.

"Adele was home," Halley was saying now. "Standing in the driveway, watching it burn. I saw her—"

And she probably saw you, Po thought, trying to put the distressing consequences out of her mind. She sat down across from Halley and listened while she finished telling Jed how she'd run away, frightened and unsure of what to do.

Eleanor had put on a pot of tea and placed a cup down in front of Halley, along with a pot of cream. "This will warm you, dear," she said. "Jed, I think I'll bring you a stiff drink."

Jed smiled his thanks.

Halley took a sip of the tea. "I didn't mean to interrupt your party, Po. I just, well, I knew Jed was working and I didn't know where else to go. And it was all so awful, seeing those flames."

"Po's door is always open, Halley," Kate said. "This was a good choice. And you're not interrupting anything. In fact,

Po left you a message to stop by if you were hungry, but couldn't reach you. Jed can tell you—he's been to Sam's Sunday suppers. Everyone is welcome."

Jed took the drink that Eleanor handed him and smiled his thanks. "Sam's suppers have pulled me through some lonely times in the past. And this would have been a safer place for Halley to be tonight, that's for sure." He looped an arm around the couch behind her. "Halley wanted to help—and also to make sure that in her grief, Adele didn't throw away things she'd be sorry about later. But I don't think Adele is there yet. I don't think she can let other people in."

Po agreed. "She's starting to let her defenses down a little, but you're right, Jed. It's going to take her awhile." Po could see the color coming back into Halley's cheeks as they talked.

"I know I shouldn't have gone over there," Halley said, her voice stronger now. "Jed told me not to. He said it would only make Adele angry. But I thought she'd be reasonable."

"You and Ollie were very close," Kate said.

Halley nodded. "I loved him. Not in a romantic, get-married kind of way. But we had a kind of spiritual connection," she said. "We read to each other and wrote poems together. We shared out thoughts. I've never been able to do that with anyone before. But Ollie was different. And he knew I appreciated that he was different and didn't condemn him for it. And he did the same for me."

The sound of the back door slamming announced that

Max was back. He walked through the open kitchen, poured himself a cup of coffee and joined them near the fireplace. "It's under control," he said. "P.J. stayed on to talk with the police."

"Police?" Po said.

"The fire wasn't an accident," Max said. The words were spoken carefully.

Po's head jerked up. "They're sure?"

Halley's eyes filled her oval face. "Oh, no," she murmured. One hand covered her mouth.

Jed's arm dropped to her shoulder and he moved closer.

"Yes, they're sure," Max said. "It was definitely arson. But only Joe's apartment was affected. The garage below wasn't badly damaged. Whoever did it wasn't very adept at lighting fires if the goal was to burn the whole estate down. The breezeway leading to the house was only mildly burned."

"How is Adele?" Eleanor asked.

Max was quiet for a moment. He wrapped his fingers around the warm mug of coffee. When he spoke, he chose his words carefully. "Adele was certainly upset. A murder in her backyard and a fire within one single weekend is enough to shake the most stalwart of folks."

Po listened and nodded. She couldn't imagine what Adele must be feeling right now, and she wondered if this might be the final straw. Would Adele call it quits, sell the property, and move away to another life that didn't include murder and fires and someone threatening her dog? She certainly couldn't blame her if she did.

Max placed his mug on the old coffee table that filled the space between the two overstuffed sofas. He reached over to touch Halley's hand. "Halley, this isn't what you need tonight, but I need to tell you this."

Halley pressed closer into Jed's side, but she looked directly into Max's eyes.

Po could tell that Halley wasn't going to be surprised at what Max would say, though she was dreading the words.

"Adele told the police that she saw a woman running away from the garage," he said. "She didn't name you. But she described you, from your brown hair, down to your Canterbury tee shirt."

Halley's eyes were dry now, her face composed and her look, level and direct. "And I saw Adele, Max," she said. "I saw her standing in the driveway as straight as an arrow, calmly staring up at the flames lapping at the side of the carriage house. That's what I saw."

CHAPTER 18

It was Phoebe who called the impromptu meeting of the Queen Bees for Monday night. The emails went out first thing Monday morning and the tone was insistent. *Meet at Selma's at seven tonight. Bring your quilt, your spirit, and your desire to turn our town back into a safe place for my babies!*

Po wasn't sure if it was Phoebe's dismay at missing the excitement of Sunday night that precipitated her action— she rarely missed a Sunday dinner—or simply her big heart and desire to help Halley Peterson out of the mess she'd fallen in to.

But she knew it was more than her desire to put the finishing stitches on Adele Harrington's quilts.

The Bees worked better with food, so Kate brought a fettuccini salad sprinkled with freshly grated parmesan cheese, fresh dill, and crisp, grilled vegetables, Po brought leftover apple pie, and Eleanor brought two chilled bottles of Chablis. While Selma plugged in the coffee pot, Po gave an abbreviated account of the fire.

"So poor Halley is under suspicion now?" she asked when Po was finished.

"Yes, but poor Halley is a strong woman under her vulnerable façade. By the time she and Jed left my house, she was composed and ready to let the police know that she was the woman Adele spotted running away—but that she had absolutely nothing to do with the fire." Po pushed her glasses up into her hair and began taking finished blocks out of her soft carrying case. "P.J. thought that was best, and he and Jed are both going to the station with her this morning."

"The thought of Halley trying to burn down Adele's home is crazy," Maggie said. "What possible reason would she have for doing that?" Maggie positioned her cutting mat, picked up her rotary cutter, and began slicing through strips of bright blue fabric for her binding.

"Be sure to use double bias binding for these quilts," Selma said, taking a pin out of her mouth. "They're going to be used a lot and will hold up better."

Phoebe looked with dismay at the single binding she had begun to stitch on her quilt.

"No problem, Phoebe dear," Selma said. "But the crib

quilt will especially need it because it will get lots of washings. We can fix that in a jiffy." She lifted the quilt from Phoebe's hands.

Leah poured herself a cup of coffee and sat down next to Maggie. The long, thick oak table was filled with strips of binding materials in a multitude of colors. Most of the tops for the B&B quilts, as the group called them, were ready for their bindings. "The talk at the college today was all about the fire and Joe's murder. Parents are calling, wondering if there's a psycho on the loose. 210 Kingfish Drive is too close to the campus for comfort."

"It's too close to all of us for comfort," Po said. "It's got to stop. I'm beginning to wonder if it's safe to walk at night, and I've never felt that way before in all the years I've lived in Crestwood."

"Are there any leads, Kate?" Phoebe asked.

All heads turned toward Kate. As P.J.'s soul mate, she sometimes had news the papers hadn't latched onto yet. Kate stood near the window, coffee in her hand and wearing a loose white blouse and slender jeans. The lights from the lamp posts lit streaks of red in her thick hair. Kate shook her head. "Not that P.J. has shared. But I know he's worried because of what it's doing to the town—and to the people involved. The longer this festers, the more damage it does to people's lives."

"We need to do something. This bed and breakfast is the future home of our quilts, ladies," Phoebe said, pushing back her chair and rising to her full 4 feet 10 inches. "What are we going to do about it?"

Kate laughed at Phoebe's gusto but admitted that

she was right. "P.J. said arson cases are often helped along by people calling in tips, things they saw that night."

Susan walked over to the iron and began pressing a binding strip. "Unfortunately what was seen was Halley. The morning news interviewed several neighbors—it was such a nice night that many people were sitting out on their porches—and the person they described seeing sounded like Halley. Apparently she wandered around the neighborhood after leaving Adele's."

"But if I hadn't been at Po's, it could have been me they saw," Kate said. "I walk through that neighborhood all the time. This is a walking town—" She gathered her thick loose hair in one hand and pulled an elastic hair band around it, then tossed it back over her shoulder. "Halley didn't try to burn that house down. I'm just sure of that."

"But she was over there, trying to get inside. Why?" Phoebe asked.

Po listened and realized she'd been wondering the same thing. She hadn't slept easily, thoughts of the burning garage and images of Joe's body still burdening her thoughts. Halley's reason for going over to Joe's was logical enough on the surface, but something about it didn't sit right. Breaking into someone's home, even if you had a key, was a serious thing. And Halley was a smart woman. And even Jed had warned her against it, someone you'd think she'd have listened to.

"Adele came to the clinic to get Emerson today," Maggie said. "That's odd, don't you think? That she boarded her dog the day of the fire? Then picked him up the day after? What was that about?"

There was silence, as eight minds pondered Adele's action. As hard as she tried, Po couldn't come up with a logical explanation. Emerson was the only thing Adele seemed to care about. The one thing she would want to protect in case of a fire.

"But why would she set fire to her own house?" Leah asked.

"Maybe there was some incriminating evidence against her in Joe's things," Phoebe offered.

"But she lives there, for heaven's sake," Eleanor said. "All she had to do was go up in the apartment and find whatever she wanted and destroy it."

There was silence as they all sorted through the conflicting motives and actions.

Selma walked over to the sideboard and filled a small plate with Kate's pasta. "Sorry, friends, I can't wait." She sat down in an old rocking chair near the food table. "Adele came in here today after she picked up Emerson. She asked how the quilts were coming. But that wasn't why she really came in."

Po looked over at Selma. "No, I don't suspect it was." The two of them and Eleanor were the only ones who knew Adele in more than a very casual way. And without discussing it, she knew Selma was sharing the same sentiments that were weighing heavily on her heart. Adele wanted to talk with someone. Wanted help.

"She didn't say much, of course," Selma went on. "But she wanted to, I could tell. She looked so terribly sad, but couldn't express it or ask for help. Adele is so self-contained that letting someone in just might cause all that glass around her to shatter."

That was so true, Po thought. And so terribly sad. *What would she have done without friends and shoulders to lean on when Sam had died?*

"This pasta is great, Kate," Maggie said, standing near the table. "Selma, I had that same feeling about Adele. She looked so sad today. Not guilty, really. Just sad. She was even nice to the office staff."

"But the truth of it is, we have to be logical about it," Phoebe said, grabbing a pad of paper from the old secretary Selma used to do her paperwork. "We know in our hearts she didn't do it, or at least we think she didn't. But okay, everyone, think this through with me." Phoebe began scribbling on the paper: *Adele—motive*.

Susan looked up. "With Ollie gone, Adele inherited the house," Susan said. "That's motive. And she had said in front of all of us that she wanted Joe gone."

"But the fire. Why the fire?" Selma asked. "That doesn't make sense."

"Insurance money?" Maggie said.

"Of course!" Phoebe said, her fingers moving across the paper. "Mags, you're super smart. She will have money to redo the carriage house now."

And the remodeling money was running low, Po thought. That much Max had shared with her the night before. Adele was worried, he had said, because she wanted the bed and breakfast to be absolutely perfect. But Po held her thoughts to herself. There was enough on Phoebe's pad already to condemn the poor woman. Could she possibly have killed her own flesh and blood? The thought caused tiny goosebumps to line up along her arms and Po rubbed them lightly, forcing the moment to pass.

"Okay," Phoebe said. "Moving on—Tom Adler. We know he thinks Ollie was going to let him have first bids on buying 210 Kingfish Drive when he died. Tom's business is in deep trouble, so my Jimmy tells me. Tom's glamorous wife is a friend of Meredith's—Jimmy's mom—and she told me that the Adlers had to give up their membership in the Crestwood Country Club last month." Phoebe laughed at the thought, a light, delicious ripple that she couldn't hold in.

"Phoebe, shame on you," Kate said, smiling at her friend and knowing that Phoebe would like nothing better than to relinquish her membership in the Crestwood Country Club. All the Bees knew Phoebe's relationship with her wealthy mother-in-law was a precarious one. Though she tried to get along because she knew the Mellons genuinely loved their grandchildren, Phoebe didn't fit comfortably into the their elegant lifestyle.

Phoebe shook her short platinum hair. "No, all's I'm saying is that Tom's pretty wife really likes her house and jewelry and all the things she's gotten used to. And Tom is nuts about her, Meredith says, and he'll stop at nothing to keep her happy."

"Stop-at-nothing—write that down, Phoebe," Maggie ordered.

"But what about Joe Bates? And the fire?" Eleanor said.

"I suppose different people could have done these things, but it doesn't seem likely."

"Maybe it was as callous as this: Joe's murder and the fire, and, God forbid, whatever awful thing comes next, are intended to make Adele's business fail and drive her out of town," Eleanor said.

"Leaving the property free for Adler's company to develop," Maggie finished.

Phoebe wrote furiously.

"And then there's Halley Peterson," Kate said. "Poor Halley, thrown right into the middle of all this."

"But doesn't seem so innocent, maybe, when you look at the facts," Leah said. "Halley was also told the house would be hers someday. I know Ollie liked her very much. Let's suppose he had told her she was in his will." Leah's words lacked conviction.

"Well, okay," Po said. "But she would never kill Joe."

"How do you know, Po? All you know about her relationship with Joe is what she's told you. Did she really like the guy? Who knows? She clearly wanted something from him, she admitted that herself," Maggie said.

"And she was seen running away from the burning garage," Leah said. "And none of us can quite buy her intense desire to get into that apartment for sentimental reasons. What was that all about?"

Phoebe stepped in. "And, she didn't much care for Adele, that we do know. Maybe she thought Adele killed Ollie and was getting even? Burning the place down would certainly accomplish that." Phoebe's words tumbled out.

She looked over at Po and noticed the deep frown lining her forehead. Phoebe waved a hand through the air. "Oh, Po, we all like Halley. I met her the other day in the library when they had a reading hour for kids, and she was so sweet to Jude and Emma. This is all hypothetical. We have to put everything down." She looked over at Eleanor. "El, I think we all need to have a glass of your wine—"

"There are also people at the college who wanted that property every bit as badly as Tom Adler did," Leah said. "Who knows what kinds of deals they had tried to work out with Oliver? I know for a fact he had made an appointment to see the chancellor—I was in the office when he came in and made it, and if I'm not mistaken, it was set up for the day after he was murdered." Leah pinched her brows together as she searched back in her memory. "Yes, I'm positive it was that day. Ollie was agitated and seemed distracted when I tried to talk to him. It was unlike him. Something was clearly on his mind and he seemed disturbed that the chancellor would talk to him right at that moment. And then, that night he died. Maybe there actually was an agreement with the college regarding the house, and he was going to cancel it." Leah was talking about her own college family now, and her voice was soft and unconvincing.

Po accepted a glass of wine from Eleanor. The timing was certainly suspicious, but from what Po knew of Ollie, he could have been meeting with the Chancellor for something very minor. Little things sometimes agitated Ollie, like computers that didn't work or classes that got cancelled. And he wouldn't have hesitated to go to the highest authority he could think of to solve the problem. "Phoebe, dear," she said aloud, "we need to be careful with all this. These are terrible things that have happened. And even being hypothetical like this puts us in a certain amount of danger."

Po looked over at her goddaughter as she spoke. Kate and Phoebe were sometimes double-trouble when trying to protect someone they liked or when they thought things were moving too slowly. Their actions were born of generous spirits, but they worried Po, nevertheless. She was fond of Phoebe, and she loved Kate as much as her own three children. Moreover, she'd vowed to Kate's mother before she died that she'd watch over her daughter, no matter what. Kate's free spirit made that difficult sometimes.

"Po, I can read your thoughts," Kate said softly, coming up beside her godmother. She put a hand on Po's shoulder and squeezed it slightly. "You have P.J. on your side, too, you know, and he warns me to mind my own business at every turn."

Po smiled up at Kate and sipped her wine. Kate's words were sincere, she knew. But at the other end of the room, Phoebe was printing their hypothesizing on an erase-board that Selma used for teaching. And Po knew she wouldn't be able to relax completely until the murderer was found. Both because she wanted the innocent to be able to get on with their lives. And because she wanted those she loved, safe.

CHAPTER 19

Po's Tuesday calendar was filled to the brim. And the only way to approach a day filled with errands and book research and a conference call with her publisher was to get up early and hit the road with a nice slow run.

Po turned off the alarm, lifted her legs over the side of the bed and stretched. In minutes she had slipped into bright green jogging pants and a Trolley Run tee shirt, downed a glass of fresh orange juice, and with Hoover at her side, headed down the shady street.

Po loved this time of day, but early as it was, the streets

weren't empty. The fall semester was in full swing and passing her frequently with polite, indulgent nods were swarms of coeds, reminding Po of the speed of bodies several generations younger than her own.

But my speed is just fine, Po thought as she continued her comfortable pace through the winding leaf-strewn streets that wrapped around the college. Hoover ran at her side, always attentive, his golden fur flying in the breeze. As Po neared the Kingfish Drive intersection, she took an unplanned turn and headed down the long shady street that housed the Harrington mansion. She would tell Eleanor later that she hadn't planned that route. But something, somehow, pulled her to the wide gated entrance of 210 Kingfish Drive. Hoover was the one who spotted the form on the driveway. And in the same instant, both Po and Hoover heard a frantic barking. In a flash, Hoover was gone, racing up the long Harrington driveway. Po followed quickly, calling to Hoover to stop. But instinct reigned over command, and in seconds Hoover stood near the figure of Adele Harrington, crumpled up beside the steps leading to the charred carriage house apartment. Emerson stood beside her, vigilant, and keeping Hoover at a respectable distance with a low growl.

"Adele!" Po reached her a minute later and crouched down beside her. "What happened? Are you all right?"

Adele was grasping her ankle, her face white and shadowed with pain. "Oh, Po," she began, an artificial bravado forced into her voice. And in the next instant, the always-composed body of Adele Harrington collapsed into ceaseless sobs. Emerson wedged his way in between Po and Adele and began licking his master's face.

Po rubbed the dog's head, then wrapped her arms around Adele's shaking shoulders and held her while tears ran down her cheeks. Finally the sobs subsided, and Adele reached for the tissue Po pulled from her pocket. "What a fool I am," she said softly.

"Your ankle is swelling, Adele. Let me help you into the house."

Adele forced a smile to her face. "Thank you," she said and allowed Po to reach beneath her arms and help her to an upright position. "I fell, you see. Foolish me. Couldn't sleep. So Emerson and I took an early walk around the grounds." She hobbled beside Po to the back door leading to the kitchen.

Po braced Adele as she pushed open the door and helped her inside. Emerson and Hoover, their sniffing of one another complete, followed.

Po pulled a chair from the table and carefully settled Adele on the cushioned seat, then pulled out another for her throbbing foot.

"Now, let's see if I can remember my first aid training," Po said, grabbing a stack of towels from the counter and positioning Adele's injured ankle on the soft cushion. Gently she moved her ankle to make sure there was nothing broken, then carefully pressed the skin around her foot.

Adele, with Emerson's head resting in her lap, wiggled her toes. "I don't think there's anything broken, Po," she said.

"I don't either. But you have a nasty sprain."

Po went to the sink, poured Adele a glass of water and spotted a bottle of acetaminophen on the windowsill. She handed two small pills to Adele. "Take these for now—it will help the pain, and I'll run you over to the emergency room when it has settled down some."

Adele shook her head. "Not necessary, Po. I can tell it's a sprain."

Po found a bowl in the cupboard and filled it with ice from the freezer, while Adele directed her to an ice bag in the butler's pantry. Po filled it, wrapped it in a towel, and gently placed it on her ankle.

"How did you fall, Adele?" Po pulled out another chair and sat beside her.

Adele took a drink of water and set the glass down on the table. Perspiration dotted her brow. She wiped it away with the back of her hand and sighed. "It was silly, Po. I looked up at the carriage house as I was walking with Emerson and realized I was going to have to go in there at some point, see what could be salvaged. And as long as I was up, I might as well be doing something. So Emerson and I started up the stairs. But I tripped and fell. Clumsy. Foolish."

"No, Adele. Neither of those. But certainly unfortunate."

Adele reached for a Kleenex from a box on the table. She dabbed at her eyes. "Thank you, Po. It was nice of you to stop."

Po smiled. "You can thank Hoover. He spotted you as we were out for a run."

"You run in the morning, Po? I used to run, when I lived back east."

"You should start again." Po looked at her ankle. "Well, maybe not for awhile. But when you're feeling better, I'll stop by someday, and we can run together. It's beautiful down by the river early in the morning."

Adele looked at her carefully, her eyes clearing. "Why are you being so kind to me? I haven't been very nice to you."

"It's not calculated, Adele, I promise. After all that's happened lately, you are probably suspicious of anyone who speaks to you."

Adele managed a slight laugh. "And anyone I speak to is suspicious of me. I know what people think, Po."

"People are frightened, Adele, that's all. We're a quiet town, quiet neighborhoods. And anything that disrupts our lives makes people nervous and wary. It's the curse and blessing of small town living."

"How could anyone think I'd kill my twin brother?" she asked suddenly.

Po shook her head. "I don't know, Adele. But you swept down on us so suddenly, took over this house, after not being here for such a long time. People don't know what to think."

"And what do you think, Po?" Adele's shoulders stiffened with the question. She looked directly into Po's eyes.

"I don't think you killed Ollie, Adele. And I don't think you killed Joe Bates or set fire to that garage, though you've given people reason to believe you might harm Joe."

"That's nonsense." Adele's voice became stronger as she spoke. But the familiar edge was softened. "Joe Bates and I never got along. Even when I was a child. He loved Ollie and he loved my mother, but I was always a nuisance to him. I know he watched over Ollie—my mother charged him with his care—and that was a good thing. But when I came back and Ollie was gone, but he was still here along with all those memories, I was resentful, I think. Irrationally so, perhaps. And I took out my frustration on him. But God knows I didn't kill him."

Adele lowered her head and Po could see the moisture return to her eyes.

When she spoke again, there was sadness coating her words. "I guess I resented him for doing what I didn't do—being here for Ollie. Helping him after my mother died. All those things. Seeing him everyday made it worse."

"Well, he did a good job of caring for Ollie, Adele, so you can take solace in that. He was a good friend to him."

"And I think he understood him better than I ever did."

The sound of a truck on the driveway broke into their conversation, and Po rose to look out the window above the sink. "Workmen," she said to Adele.

"Yes," Adele answered.

Po watched her as she took another drink of water, wondering if Adele would be able to manage here by herself. Without her make-up and fine clothes, Adele looked younger, and even though her face registered discomfort, she looked oddly beautiful. Gone was the stony façade that kept people at a distance, the piercing look that caused others to look away or shift their weight from one foot to another. But also gone was the appearance of someone who was totally self-sufficient and impervious to outside forces.

Adele Harrington looked vulnerable.

"Po," Adele said, looking up from her chair. "Po, do you think—"

Po waited, but the sentence hung there in the air for so long, Po thought for a minute Adele had forgotten what she was going to ask. "Yes?" she finally prompted.

"Po, do you think it's time I threw in the towel?"

For a minute, Po wasn't sure what Adele was asking. And then as she followed her gaze around the room, the big, beautiful old home, she realized what Adele was suggesting.

"And move away, you mean? Sell the home, pack up your dream?"

Adele nodded slowly. "I'm a strong woman, Po. I've had to be independent for a long time. My mother urged me out of this house and into a world in which women had the disadvantage. But I've always held my own. Always."

Po listened as Adele continued. "This house was never mine, you know. Coming back after Ollie died, I thought maybe I could make it a lovely place, make it mine. Fill it with people. Pull up the memories I have that are good, bury the others. I thought I could bring back my mother and my brother somehow, adding beauty to this place they loved."

"And you can, Adele. It's going to be a magnificent place."

"But what is happening around me? Someone doesn't want me here, Po. Someone wants this house in a terrible, insane way. And how many people will be hurt while I stubbornly hang on to it?" Adele winced as she tried to shift in the chair.

"Adele, you can't let others rule your life." Po walked over to the sink and poured herself a glass of water. She looked out at the workman pulling ladders and toolboxes from their truck. She saw a gardener take a wheelbarrow from the garage, and in the distance, she heard someone whistling a light sweet tune. She turned from the sink and felt an enormous resolve.

"Adele," Po said. "You can't let anyone take this away from you. This is your home. Somehow, I promise you, we will bring an end to the bad things happening here. And you will be at home again. Now let's get on with it."

CHAPTER 20

Despite the fact that gossip sometimes ran rampant in Crestwood, when push came to shove, it was a place where neighbors looked out for neighbors. And when Po made a call to Leah's husband, Tim, at his busy pediatric practice and asked him to stop by on his way home to check the sprained ankle of a fifty-two-year-old woman, she knew the favor would be granted.

"She'll be fine, Po," Tim assured her when he called later that evening. "Adele has a couple of crutches to help her around for the next few days, but she's one determined lady, and I don't think anything as minor as a fat ankle will keep her down for long."

Po smiled into the phone at the description of Adele. She was a strong lady, for sure. But she also had a soft spot. And Po suspected that it would certainly widen in time and allow more people in.

"By the way, Po," Tim added. "Leah mentioned to me that Adele had boarded her dog the day of the fire and it was raising some eyebrows. Sounded suspicious, I guess."

"Yes?" Po had not addressed that with Adele herself. But she knew—she hoped—there was a reason, because Tim was correct—it was very suspicious.

"Well, she mentioned to me that she had had the yard sprayed," Tim said. "She wondered if I thought she was being overly protective by not wanting Emerson around the chemicals. I told her no, that I thought she was one wise lady. Those chemicals are awful for dogs—and kids," Tim added, before hanging up the phone.

For a brief moment, Po felt a wash of shame for doubting Adele's motives. And then great relief, and then she grinned and moved on with her phone calls.

A call to Eleanor assured Po that Adele would have food the next day. Eleanor would stop by 210 Kingfish Drive the next day with groceries, a stack of her travel magazines, and a deck of cards. And Kate said she'd check in on Adele periodically as she jogged by the house on her daily runs.

And Po herself would help out by donning an old pair of jeans and a Canterbury sweatshirt, and begin rummaging through the charred remains of Joe's apartment, saving Adele the grief of doing so herself.

"Thank you, Po," Adele said when Po showed up the next Thursday morning. "I don't know why you are all pitching in like this. But I—"

"Oh, shush," Po said. "It's what we do."

"Well, you do it well," Adele allowed. She sat in a sunroom just off the kitchen, her foot wrapped in a flesh-colored bandage and elevated on a small stool. Windows surrounded her on three sides, and she could easily monitor the activity and comings and goings of the workman without moving an inch. To the side, spread out on a low coffee table, were piles of papers, forms, and a laptop computer.

"This looks like command central, Adele." The color had come back into Adele's high cheekbones, and she was dressed comfortably today in loose, soft slacks and a silky teal-green blouse. She looked quite beautiful, Po thought.

Adele nodded. "They don't know it, but with that window open," Adele nodded to a window next to the couch, "I can hear everything they say. It's an education, believe me."

"I've no doubt." Po laughed.

"But the sad thing is," Adele continued, watching the men beyond her window, "some of them are refusing to come to work. The crew has diminished considerably in the past week."

Po frowned. "I wasn't aware of that."

"They don't want to be connected to what's happening here. They hate it that television cameras stop by and film them. But the real reason, I know, is that they hear the rumors, too. They know that some people think I killed Joe—and there are even some who think I killed my brother. I can't say I blame the workmen for not wanting to be here. But I can't afford to be without them. Every delay costs me money."

There was genuine sadness shadowing Adele's face, and Po had a powerful urge to find the contractor and give him a piece of her mind. *Whatever happened to innocent until proven guilty?* Aloud, she said, "Would you like some coffee before I tackle the carriage house?"

Adele shook her head no. "I don't know how bad it is up there, Po, but it should be safe. The fireman said they were able to control it before the foundation was weakened." She looked across the drive at the open windows and charred sills of the garage apartment, then back at Po. "If it's too awful and the smell is too bad, please don't stay. I don't think there's much of value up there, Po. My mother filled the place with old cast-off books from our library, hoping Joe Bates might educate himself. He never seemed very interested though. All I really care about are things of Oliver's—please save them for me. Contrary to that librarian's rantings, I would never have thrown anything of my brother's away."

"I think Halley is still emotional over Oliver's death, Adele. I don't think she means those things."

"Oh, Po, that's where you're wrong. She means them.

But for the life of me, I don't know where her accusations are coming from."

Po picked up her work gloves. She didn't want to argue with Adele. Besides, she had a point. Halley did seem to attack Adele rather severely. That was one of the things Po intended to ask Halley about when she had a chance. That, and what the young woman thought she could possibly find in Joe's apartment that was worth trespassing and angering Adele. Perhaps spending a little time in the carriage house herself would shed some light on Halley's obsession with it. "Well, I'm off," she said to Adele. "You can call me on my cell phone if you need anything. I've left the number there beside your computer."

Adele waved her hand in the air. "I'm fine, Po. I get around quite nicely on these crutches—and they make nice battering poles should anyone give me trouble."

Po took several plastic bags from the kitchen, then walked across the driveway and up the back steps of the carriage house. It was a bright, crisp fall day, and the clean air was a sharp contrast to the awful stench on the other side of Joe Bates' door. Po walked in cautiously, feeling the presence of the old man who had kept to himself so severely these past years.

Light from the open windows revealed a soot-filled, damp room with a small galley kitchen at one end. Off to one side, Po walked into a room with a bed and dresser, cluttered now with burnt ceiling tiles scattered everywhere.

Remnants of barely recognizable personal items—a hair-brush and floppy hat, books, and a reading lamp—lay like clumps of coal on the floor. Here and there small puddles of water remained, reminders of the firemen's attack against the flames. And everywhere was the pungent odor of burnt matter.

Joe's place must have been cozy before the fire racked such havoc, Po thought, walking back into the living room and looking around. Built-in blackened bookcases filled an interior wall, and a small brass telescope lay on its side on a table near a window. A gift from Oliver, Po suspected.

Some things escaped the flames, Po noticed, but almost nothing escaped the force of the water that put them out. An old, overstuffed chair and couch, pushed now to the center of the room, was wet and lumpy, burned on one side but not the other. Po sighed. The remains of a long life reduced to rubble. The sadness that came over her was unexpected—and profound.

To work, she told herself. *There will be time for dealing with sad thoughts later.*

After slipping on her work gloves, Po walked carefully to the bookcase, stepping over broken dishes and burnt dishtowels, black flakes of newspapers and chunks of canned food that had exploded from the heat.

Some of the shelves held nothing but charred clumps of the Harrington's old books that Adele had mentioned. But on other shelves, the books were still recognizable. She carefully pulled one from the shelf and read the darkened spine. It was Rudyard Kipling's *Jungle Book*, and she tried to think of old Joe, sitting in his chair by the window, reading it. Perhaps Adele was wrong and Joe Bates read avidly, devouring these classics. One never knew everything about another's life, and the thought of Joe steeping himself in reading pleased Po. You could learn so much about a per-son from the books they read, she thought. She set the book on the floor near her stash of garbage sacks, thinking it might be salvageable—and perhaps even a collector's item.

For an hour Po rummaged through books and charred papers, scattered across the shelves and on the floor. She collected those that were still intact and made a small pile near the door, then added some framed pictures of Oliver and his mother that were wavy beneath the glass but still intact. There was a picture of Oliver and Joe, and one of a young Oliver—perhaps twenty or so—standing next to a beautiful young woman. Po took it over to the window and looked at it more closely in the sunlight, rubbing the surface clean with her finger. Only in the bright natural light did Po realize the woman was Adele. She was stand-ing next to her brother, smiling into the camera. Po took a piece of paper towel and rubbed the cracked glass. Adele and Ollie. Happy. Po wrapped the picture in folds of paper towel to protect it and added it to her pile.

A solid old roll-top desk, its legs darkened by the fire but still holding up the top, stood a few feet from the book-shelf. It was a massive thing, Po saw, and seemed to have resisted the fire by its very boldness. The curved roll-top, swollen with water and singed by flames, stuck when Po tried to slide it up, but a few strong tugs and it gave way. Inside, Po found more of Joe's life—pads of paper, damp bills, pens and pencils, and several small books. Some legal-looking documents that were waterlogged and curled. Po pressed one flat and could read Ollie's name at the bottom, but the rest was smeared and indecipherable. Po frowned. Odd. And somewhat unsettling. Po thought about all the claims on Oliver's house, and the thought that he may have written up a will before he died surfaced briefly, then disappeared beneath the weight of the task in front of her. Po gathered what papers were intact and set them beside the door to look at later.

Po emptied the cubby-hole containers in the old desk and found bank books and scraps of papers, a small garden guide filled with newspaper clippings on gardening and notes Joe must have written to himself. She picked up a still-intact book jacket, soggy now and darkened from heat. *A Plain Man's Guide to a Starry Night.* She smiled at the thought of Joe reading the book, maybe sitting by the window, looking up at the night sky that Jed had written about in his book. Clearly, Adele was wrong. Joe did read. And read books that Ollie would have liked, perhaps that Ollie had encouraged his friend to read.

Po piled the desk contents into a box and continued poking though the cavernous lower cabinet of the old desk, pulling out more pictures, an old pipe that still had tobacco packed tightly inside the bowl, and a whole stack of legal-sized yellow pads of paper. Po smiled at the pads. She and Joe had something in common—capturing thoughts on yellow pads of paper. Po had them lying all over her house. She picked one up and realized it was Ollie's, his familiar, neat printing filling the lines. Notes from a class, it looked like, and another cited books from the library, and in the margin of one, she spotted Halley's name and a small heart doodled next to it. *This is the kind of thing Halley must have been looking for*, she thought. The things she had shared with Ollie and that Joe had taken from his room before Adele arrived. Po scooped up the pads and added them to her stash. Perhaps she would give Halley the pad with her name on it—a small reminder of how much Ollie cared about her. It would mean something to Halley, and Adele surely wouldn't want it.

A few hours later, Po decided she had done all she could do and the rest could be done by workmen who would remove the debris and prepare the small apartment for its renovation. She hailed a painter walking behind the house and had him help her pile the salvageable things in boxes— the telescope and a couple of lamps that had escaped the fire's wrath. Some silverware that might have been Adele's mother's. Po decided Adele should see them and decide their fate. She directed the painter to carry some of the boxes over to the house, storing them for now in the basement where the smell wouldn't bother Adele.

The other things—the desk contents, some books, a pile of photographs and the yellow pads—she piled in boxes and carried to her car. She'd dry them out at home and return to Adele anything that might have memories of Ollie attached to it.

A day's work well done, she thought, driving down the driveway and tugging her cell phone from the pocket of her jeans. She was pleased that she had relieved Adele of a task that would clearly be a burden to her.

And now that the Adele was settled and the carriage house was cleaned out, there were other things Po needed to put her mind to. Phoebe, bless her platinum head, was right this time. Things were moving too slowly, and a woman's reputation was at stake—and maybe her life. Something had to be done soon to salvage Adele Harrington's reputation—and the beautiful bed and breakfast inn at 210 Kingfish Drive.

Po paused at the end of the drive and pushed the buttons on her small silver phone. "P.J.," she said out loud. "How wonderful that I've caught you. How would you like to share a bowl of spicy shrimp soup with me tonight?"

C H A P T E R   2 1

"I'm only here because of your cooking, Po," P.J. said, standing over the stove and stirring the rich coconut milk broth. He closed his eyes and breathed in the pungent smell of garlic, ginger, and parsley. "It's definitely not the fact that I strongly suspect I'm being lured here for other, less delicious motives."

Po smiled and spread two placemats out on the oak table that had been the heart of the Paltrow home for thirty years. Small indentations along the surface spoke of years of homework, games being played, and friends gathering to argue politics, literature, and philosophies of life while eating and drinking in the warmth of the Paltrow family room.

"Better set three, Po," P.J. said, glancing at the table.

"Kate knows you're here?"

P.J. nodded. He scooped up a small amount of soup in a ladle and tasted it. "This is fantastic. You've outdone yourself, Po." He set the spoon in the sink and walked across the kitchen to the small bar in the family room bookcase and began mixing gin and ice cubes in a silver shaker. "Kate doesn't care about me, Po," he said over his shoulder. "It's your Thai soup."

Po pulled out another placemat. She had purposely not called Kate because she didn't want her around when she talked to P.J. about the murders. But that was silly, she knew. Kate had never fit nicely in a cocoon, and Po's instinct to put her there whenever there was a chance of anything bordering on danger or sadness was irrational, if heart-felt. And there was always plenty of food—she'd made enough soup for an army, planning on taking some over to Adele the next day and freezing the rest.

"Kate had a yearbook meeting with the high school kids but will be here when it's over. She was skipping pizza for your Thai soup."

"I'm honored," Po said. The sound of a car in the driveway announced Kate's possible arrival, but when Po looked over at the back door, it was Leah coming in, a deep rust corduroy skirt swishing around her ankles and a hand-woven scarf wrapped around her neck. And just a step behind her was Jed Fellers.

"It's getting chilly out there," Leah said, taking off a wool jacket and hanging it on a hook by the door. "I hope you don't mind my barging in, Po. Jed and I had a committee meeting, and I convinced him that the only antidote for it was a bowl of that Thai soup you told me you were making tonight. Tim was on call, and I needed to be with people." She waved across the room at P.J. and gave Po a hug. "And I convinced Jed that he did, too."

Behind her, Jed smiled sheepishly. "Hope it's okay, Po. Leah was hard to say no to."

"Of course I don't mind," Po said, smelling the bouquet of flowers Jed handed her. "I'd have been offended if you had said no, Jed."

"I think it's all this unrest, Po," Leah went on, searching in Po's cupboard for a vase. "I feel it on campus every day. Just bad vibes everywhere."

"The kids are confused," Jed agreed. "It's a tense time." He took the vase from Leah and filled it with water.

Po pulled out a couple more placemats. "The soup will ease the chill. But you're absolutely right about the tension. The neighborhood is filled with bad energy. And, unfortunately, it's going to take more than soup to get rid of it. How is Halley handling it all, Jed?"

Jed thought for a minute before answering. He put the flowers in the vase, set it aside, and leaned back against the counter. "I think she's doing all right, Po. We're both wondering now if we'll ever know who is at the bottom of all this. And Halley is trying to accept that, trying to move on."

"I was inclined to think that myself. But the fire changed

that. It brought the presence of someone evil closer to us again, not someone who did those awful deeds, then skipped town."

"There's the possibility that they're not connected," Leah said.

Po thought about that. P.J. had told her the same thing before the others came. The police were considering all angles. But deep down, Po didn't buy it. There were connections between all the happenings at the B&B, she felt sure of it. Unfortunately, feelings didn't solve crimes. She needed some facts.

A minute later, Kate breezed through the back door, pulling it shut behind her. She strode across the kitchen and swung a lumpy cloth bag onto the counter. "Fresh French bread from Picasso's, a bottle of wine and hunk of cheese from Brew and Brie, and Marla's cheesecake. Elderberry Road in a bag," she laughed. She planted a kiss on Po's cheek and hugged Leah.

"Come here, woman," P.J. bellowed in a deep feigned accent from the other end of the room. "What am I—chopped liver?" He set down the martini shaker and spread his arms wide.

Kate walked across the room and into his embrace, wrapping her arms around his waist. Her thick dark hair brushed his cheek.

P.J. breathed in her scent. "Katie, my love, you smell almost as good as Po's soup," he murmured.

"And you smell like gin." Kate pulled her head back and looked into P.J.'s wide smile. A lock of sandy hair fell across his forehead, and Kate brushed it back with her finger. She pulled away. "I'll leave you to your shaking, Flanigan. Make mine with an olive, please." Kate moved back to the kitchen and began pulling out platters for the cheese and bread.

Po knelt down before the floor-to-ceiling stone fireplace that filled one end of the roomy living area. She pulled the black screen open. "I'm going to start a fire. I know it's early, but somehow it seems to fit the night."

"My job," Jed insisted, and knelt down beside the fireplace. "Let me put my Eagle Scout training to work."

"Perfect," Leah said, and carried the platter filled with cheese and crackers to the coffee table. "Maybe it will warm our bones a bit." She slipped out of her clunky clogs and settled down on the overstuffed couch, her feet tucked up beneath her.

Po sat down beside her and accepted a martini from P.J. "And together we'll warm each other's spirit." She sipped the martini slowly, enjoying the tingly sensation as it passed down her throat. The evening hadn't turned out exactly as she had planned—a private talk with P.J. to pull what information she could out of him about the investigation into Ollie and Joe's deaths. Even though P.J. wasn't working the case, he always knew what was going on, especially when it was as personal and close to home as this case was. She wanted an update, wanted him to know she was absolutely convinced that Adele had no part in any of the bad things that were happening in their neighborhood. She wanted him to help salvage what was left of a proud woman's reputation.

Kate stepped into her thought. "I stopped by on my way over here to check on Adele." Kate had curled up on the opposite couch, her long, jeans-clad legs twisted like a pretzel beneath her. A red cashmere sweater that Po had given her for Christmas last year matched the color the fire was bringing to her cheeks. "She's one gutsy woman. Tom Adler stopped by while I was there. That guy just doesn't give up. He left his wife out in his Beemer and barged right into the house. He suggested the time had come for Adele to sell the place before she ruined the whole town. His words, certainly not mine." Kate cut a piece of cheese and handed it to Leah.

"What?" Po sat up straight, nearly spilling her martini down the front of her black turtleneck. "What is he talking about?"

"He insinuated that Adele was personally responsible for two murders, a fire, nervous neighbors, and the loss of business to the town because people were afraid to come to Crestwood with Adele around."

"The man is certifiably crazy," Leah said.

"And desperate," P.J. said.

Jed stoked the fire until the embers were glowing and flames began lapping at the brick sides, then lifted himself into a chair nearby where he could give it a poke when needed. "Adler came into Picasso's the other night when Max and I were having a drink. He'd been drinking pretty heavily and Picasso asked him to leave. I think the fellow has some personal problems."

"He's in some financial trouble, yes, but that's no excuse

for that kind of behavior. Adele should have accused him of trespassing," Po said.

"Oh, she did," Kate said. "She threatened to call the police, and I think she would have, but the damsel waiting for Tom became impatient and began honking the horn. Tom went running."

"He's such an angry man," Leah said. "I wonder if he had anything to do with this."

"He certainly has motive," Kate said. "He's been acting crazy ever since marrying again. I think this new wife has very high expectations for him—especially when it comes to money."

"That would be enough to make someone desperate, I suppose," Po said. But she wasn't completely convinced. There was something about Tom Adler that was far more show than substance. But if not Tom—who could have murdered the two men who lived at 210 Kingfish Drive— one so gentle and almost naïve about life, and the other an old gardener whose sole goal was to protect Ollie from harm and keeping his pond free of algae?

"How about we have some soup?" P.J. announced. "It smells ready and I'm starving."

"P.J., if I ever open a restaurant, will you be my sandwich board man?" Po asked.

"Your what?" P.J. asked, wrinkling his forehead. "Po, I'm far too young to know about sandwich boards. But the answer's yes." He waved the others over. "Come on folks, get it while it's hot. Jed, want to open a bottle of wine?"

Jed helped himself to the corkscrew and Kate's bottle of wine and poured glasses all around. Po walked over to the table and the others followed, finding their chairs and unfolding napkins as Po spooned soup from the tureen into rice-filled bowls. The thick soup, a mixture of sautéed shrimp and snow peas flavored with ginger, garlic, and lime juice, and swimming in spicy coconut milk, was P.J.'s favorite.

"Where's Max tonight?" Kate asked, leaning in to light the candles.

"He was going to stop by Adele's. She's concerned because the renovation is taking longer than it should, and Max was going to look at the money situation for her." Po repeated the news about the workers slowing down and staying away, not wanting to be connected with the murder scene.

"That's awful," Kate said. "This whole thing is awful. I think Phoebe's right—we should all don black jeans and turtlenecks and snoop around until we solve this thing. I think maybe we're all going off on the wrong path with this. What if it doesn't have anything to do with someone wanting to own the Harrington property?"

"But what else makes sense?" Jed asked.

"I don't know," Kate replied. "But if teaching high school kids has taught me anything, it's that things are rarely what they seem to be."

Po had been thinking the very same thing. In all her years of living, things were rarely what they seemed. So what was going on here? What were they missing? Was it Adele herself? Was she back in Crestwood for reasons no one knew? Was there a family thing going on, something between the Harringtons and another family in town? The Adlers, perhaps? Or maybe Ollie and Joe were mixed up in something that had gotten them in trouble. Drugs? Every now and then there were rumors of people selling to the college kids. The thought was so ludicrous and uncomfortable that it made Po grimace.

"Po, are you all right?" P.J. asked. His hazel eyes focused on her face.

"Yes, dear," Po answered, brushing off his concern. She forced a smile to her face. "I was just trying to sort through some things. Dessert, anyone?"

When Max stopped by an hour later, Po's impromptu dinner companions had moved into the night—P.J. and Kate to walk along the well-lit river path while the weather still afforded such a luxury, Leah home to deliver a left-over container of soup to a tired husband. And Jed was headed to the campus library to walk Halley home from her late-night shift. Po appreciated his thoughtfulness. Halley shouldn't be out on the streets alone, not until things in Crestwood became normal again.

Po sat alone in the darkened living room, the lights dim and the dying embers of the fire casting shadows on the pine-planked floor. "Hi, Max," she said, watching her dear friend walk across the kitchen. "Please don't mind if I stay put. I'm pooped. There's leftover soup in the frig."

Max strode across the room and kissed Po on the cheek, then busied himself at the small bar. "Maybe in a minute, Po. Thanks." Max mixed himself a Scotch and soda and sat at her side. "Adele's not a bad lady, Po."

Po nodded.

"But what's happening around her is not good. Her finances are strained, the workers are making things difficult. And rumors are spreading throughout the neigh-borhood that there's a murderer in their midst."

"Who's spreading those rumors, Max?"

Max shrugged. "Some well-intentioned folks, probably— there are some elderly folks who live on that street and they are likely concerned. For a quiet neighborhood, there's a lot of unusual activity at 210 Kingfish Drive. And then there are people like the mothers in Phoebe's playgroup. And maybe a few with other motives, like Tom Adler and board members from the college who would love to get their hands on the property." Max looped an arm around the back of the couch behind Po and sipped his drink. "It's not a good situation for Adele, that's for sure. Bed and breakfasts conjure up images of cozy bedrooms and warm scones for breakfast, not fires and dead bodies floating in ponds."

Po looked into the flames, as if hoping to find an answer there. "Kate said something tonight that has me thinking, Max. She said things may not be at all what they seem to be."

"Sure. That's a possibility. If they are what they seem

to be, Adele is suspect No. 1 and Tom and Halley are probably tied for second place."

"So maybe the motive isn't greed. Maybe it isn't the property at all."

Max listened and nodded. "Maybe it's something right in front of our noses. And all we need to do is step back a bit."

In her dreams that night, Po stepped back as far as she could, and as darkness folded in around her, she felt herself falling off a cliff. Suddenly, in the blackness, she felt herself caught in strong, familiar arms. She awoke with a start, sitting up in bed, and as the fog and fear cleared from her head, Po looked up at the moonlight streaming in the window. Sam's presence was so real that Po thought for a minute
she could reach out and touch the arms that rescued her.

"So my darling," she said aloud, "what would you have me do right now?" But she knew the answer, even without Sam wrapping strong arms around her shoulders and holding her close.

My darling Po, tread lightly and safely, he'd say. And then he'd pull those thick brows together and try to look at her sternly, but the look would be more one of loving concern, tinged with great pride.

CHAPTER 22

Po was up with the first light. She plugged in her coffee pot and filled Hoover's bowl with fresh water. It was too early to approach the world beyond her doors, so she'd begin instead with what was close by, anything that would bring her closer to understanding the lives of the two men who had lived at 210 Kingfish Drive. And perhaps in understanding their lives and their friendship, she'd come closer to understanding why they had died.

And there was plenty of Joe and Ollie's lives spread out in her basement, drying in the warm furnace-heated air.

She hadn't begun to look at the things she'd brought from Adele's. It was time.

Po poured herself a cup of coffee, flicked the light switch in the hallway just off the kitchen, and headed down the narrow back stairs.

Sam and Po had finished one side of their basement as a playroom for the kids years ago, just after Sophie was born. The knotty-pine walls spoke of another era but held warm memories for Po, as did the eight-foot table that had hosted countless birthday parties, Cub Scout projects, and craft sessions. Today it was spread end-to-end with remnants of Joe Bates' carriage house apartment—pads of paper, books propped open to encourage drying, photographs and small paintings of flowers that she suspected Joe had done himself. When she'd emptied the boxes, Po had discovered that she'd brought home more than she had intended. And there was still a box that she'd forgotten in her car.

But no matter—she'd get around to it all. Spread it all out, dry it, and return to Adele what was salvageable. The pictures, especially, she knew Adele would want, and she set to work, carefully removing them from their frames, pressing them smooth, and placing them on paper towels.

Po removed the pieces of paper stuck inside books, some written on in Ollie's handwriting, which Po recognized from the things she'd seen in his room. The distinctive blend of printing and cursive was intriguing and unmistakable.

As she smoothed out the pages torn from a yellow

legal pad, Po wondered what people would find out about her if someday they went through her books and tried to interpret the underlinings, the notes in the margin, and the dozens of small pieces of paper and sticky notes she'd put in a book to save her place, or on which she'd copied a line she especially liked. Ollie had made plenty of notes on scraps of paper, perhaps intended to teach Joe, to help him understand the stars, the heavens, the things that Ollie loved. She picked up the copy of Jed's book. She'd have to pick up a copy of it one of these days. Gus mentioned he had read it and was going to order some for the store. There were notes in the column here, too. Some were washed away by the firemen's efforts, but some were still intact, with passages underlined and handwritten stars scribbled next to favorite passages. Po suspected Ollie had given Joe the book to read.

The ringing of the phone in the distance startled Po for a minute, then drew her out of her thoughts and up the basement stairs.

"Hi, Po. Are you up?" Kate's bright voice rippled across the line.

"Kate Simpson, have I ever slept beyond 7 o'clock in my life?" Po set her empty coffee cup in the sink and looked out into the deep green of her backyard as she listened to Kate. The oak leaves were beginning to turn color, and there was already a light coating of maple leaves on the ground, scattered now as Hoover chased a squirrel around a bed of mums.

"Sorry, Po," Kate said. "It seemed a logical question

when you're calling someone at eight in the morning."

"Why aren't you at school?"

"There's a teachers' conference in Kansas City. It seemed optional, so I stayed behind. I need to run by the college to pick up some books, but after that, you up for coffee? Your place?"

"Better yet, let's meet at the college. The new coffee house is carrying Peet's coffee. Give me an hour."

After she hung up the phone, Po took a quick shower and slipped into a pair of light corduroy slacks and a soft teal turtleneck. She ran a brush through her hair, then pulled it back off her face with an elastic band. A check of her e-mails and she was ready to go. She had planned a trip to Canterbury today anyway, to pick up some books and, hopefully, to run into Halley Peterson and see how she was doing. She would get back to the basement later.

Po walked the few blocks to Canterbury College—she could never get used to calling it Canterbury University— a bit pretentious, she thought. The campus was beautiful at this time of year, with giant shade trees shedding leaves and students walking briskly along the paths. Several students tossed Frisbees in the quad, and others hurried to class. Po entered the crowded coffee shop and looked around for Kate. She spotted her immediately in the corner near the front window, commandeering two leather chairs and a small round table. Po hurried over.

"Got here just in time," Kate said. "The place is a zoo with everyone wanting their start-the-day jolt of java."

Po sat down, dropped her bag beside the chair and looked around, taking stock of the crowded, early-morning crowd. Halley Peterson waved at her from her place in line across the room, and Po waved back, motioning for her to join them when she was through. "She's one of the reasons I wanted to stop by the college today," Po said, nodding toward the librarian. "You don't mind, do you, Kate?"

"Of course not. I like Halley. P.J. and I ran into her the other night on Elderberry Road. We were at Picasso's for a bowl of his bouillabaisse, and she and Jed Fellers came in for dinner. They were having a good time, I think—lots of gabbing going on and Halley had a pretty blush to her cheeks. I think difficult times can bring people together more quickly than the normal course of living."

"Halley does seem a little happier these days, though I know Ollie and Joe's deaths have taken a toll on her. I'm glad she has Jed to help her through it."

"Sometimes we forget that Jed is going through all this, too. Leah said he was so good to Ollie over the years—a true mentor."

"I know he gave Ollie a chance that others might not have done. I think even Adele acknowledges that."

At that moment, Halley walked over to their table with a coffee container in one hand and a cinnamon roll in the other. "You don't mind?" she asked, putting down her coffee and pulling over an empty chair from the wall. Her smile was bright.

"A new haircut?" Po asked, admiring Halley's shorter

cut. She had also used a new shade of lipstick, and jeans had given way to a shapely skirt and soft cashmere sweater. "You look lovely, Halley," Po said.

Halley blushed. "I've decided that shabby wasn't chic on me," she said.

"You were never shabby, but you do look great," Kate added.

"So what's new?" Halley asked, clearly anxious to divert attention from herself.

"Well, you may have heard that Adele Harrington sprained her ankle," Po began.

Halley frowned. "I didn't know that."

"She was going up to clean out Joe's place after that awful fire," Kate explained.

"Po found her."

"Did she do it?"

"Do what?" Po asked, unsure of Halley's question.

"Clean out the apartment?" Halley said.

Po was quiet for a moment, wondering why Halley seemed to skip over the more obvious and caring question about Adele's injury. Perhaps it was because Halley had fond feelings for Joe Bates—and not-so-fond ones for Adele.

Halley seemed to read Po's thoughts and said quickly, "I don't mean to seem uncaring about Adele Harrington, Po. It's just that she and I haven't seen eye-to-eye on things."

"I've noticed that," Po said. "And I understand some of it—Adele hasn't been very understanding about your friendship with her brother."

Halley ran her fingers through her hair and shook her head. When she spoke, her voice had an edge to it that Po hadn't heard before in the quiet librarian. "No, she hasn't. And I still think Adele had something to do with Ollie's death—or at least knows more about it than she's saying. If he'd lived, she would never have been able to turn the house into a bed and breakfast. Ollie said he was going to change his will—Adele wasn't even supposed to get the house."

"Who was?" Kate asked.

Halley stared at her plate. Finally she looked up. "I don't know. Not Adele. Maybe...maybe me, he said. I told him that was silly, but I don't think he had many people he was close to. And he wanted the house cared for."

"Ollie told you he had changed his will?" Po asked.

"Well, sort of."

"And that's why you think Adele had something to do with his death? That seems awfully severe, Halley. Ollie was her twin brother and her only sibling. I don't know how you can make that leap."

Halley nodded. "At first I couldn't imagine someone killing her own brother. But it happens all the time, Po. Most murders are within families." She looked at Po, then Kate. "It's true," she said. Her voice was harder now.

Po listened intently, watching belief fill Halley's eyes. Her words seemed to strengthen her resolve and the smile fell from her face as she talked.

"Well, it's not true in this case," Kate said.

"Kate, you don't know that," Halley said. "There are

things you don't know about Adele Harrington. She's greedy, she's not a good person."

"Why do you think that, Halley?" Po asked. "I know Adele is abrupt and can even be rude, but she has had an enormous amount of grief to bear these weeks. Her life has been pulled apart. I think your judgment is unduly harsh."

Halley bit down on her bottom lip, as if preventing herself from saying something she might regret. She looked at Po directly, her eyes flashing. "I believe what I believe. And I respect that you have your own convictions. You're wrong, though." She pushed back her chair and forced a smile to her face. "I better get to the library now. My shift starts in a few minutes."

Po and Kate watched as Halley dropped her napkin and paper plate into the refuse container, then took her cup and hurried out the door. From the window they saw her wave at Jed Fellers, walking down the sidewalk from the opposite direction, an armload of books in his hand and a student at his side. Jed returned her wave, and even from their distant viewing point, Kate and Po could see the concern and consternation on the woman's face fall away, and in its place was a bright look of joy.

"Now I understand the change in dress. The make-up," Kate said.

"Halley Peterson is smitten," Po finished.

"I wonder if she's shared her dislike of Adele Harrington with Jed?"

"Probably not. Jed has been supportive of Adele. I don't think Adele trusts people easily, and Jed hasn't quite received a warm welcome, but he's been gentlemanly about trying to help where he can. Oliver thought a lot of him, so it seems appropriate."

"Why do you think Halley is so concerned about Joe's apartment?" Kate asked.

"I think she just wants some remembrance of Ollie. Maybe it's purely a sentimental thing."

Kate shook her head. "It doesn't ring completely true to me, Po. Her efforts to retrieve something of Ollie's seem kind of weird. She has her memories, and surely Ollie would have given her what he wanted her to have."

"To be honest, Kate, I agree with you. I want to ask her about it, but this didn't seem the right time."

"So why, Po?" Kate nibbled on her scone. "Why has Halley continued to barge into Adele's life when she's been told to stay away?"

Po drained her cup. Why indeed. What was Halley Peterson keeping?

Po and Kate went their separate ways with promises to talk later. And if not, they'd probably see each other that night—Po and Max were taking Eleanor to Picasso's to celebrate her birthday, and Kate said she and P.J. might stop by.

But for now, Kate was heading for the park to take some pictures. And think about Ollie Harrington and Joe Bates. And Tom Adler, and Adele. She confessed to Po that she'd had dreams about them all the night before. She was walking through a forest, following Joe and Ollie. And they kept nearing the edge of the woods, where the trees fell away and sunlight flooded the earth. But they never quite reached the light. They were always an inch away. And the darkness kept getting darker.

An inch away. Po thought. She felt that, too. The pieces of the puzzle were scattered all around them. If only they could scoop them up and fit them into the right places, perhaps they could bring some closure to all this—bring some light into the darkness—before someone else got hurt.

That thought was never far from Po's mind. She was acutely aware that all the Bees were in and out of Adele's home these days. A small piece of her understood the workman's fears in being so close to a place in which two men had been murdered.

Po went home and put in a load of wash, trying to shake the awful foreboding that weighed heavy on her. She ran Hoover over to Maggie's for a check-up, then finally, later in the day, settled down in her den to work on an article she was writing for a quilting magazine. She'd been asked to write about the Queens Bees, its origins nearly half a century ago, and explain how the group wove together art and friendship. A topic close to her heart.

But after an hour of staring at an empty screen, Po ealized her mind was too full of other things, and it was futile to sit there any longer. Instead of writing, she found herself doodling on a yellow pad from the stack she kept in the den, ready to jot down ideas for books or articles or sketches for quilts. Somehow, writing down scattered thoughts sometimes made them more comprehensible. She and Ollie, perhaps, were alike in that way. Po carried the pad into the kitchen.

Ollie. Joe. she had written on the pad. People on her mind. Two good friends.

House. Apartment. It occurred to Po that dwellings figured prominently in the lives of these friends. Bound them together. She scribbled on the pad, drew circles around their names. *Halley.* She seemed to love the house almost as much as Ollie had. Perhaps that was why she loved it— because it had been his. And Halley thought Ollie had wanted her to have it. An odd thought for casual friends. But Ollie seemed to have made the promise of his house to many people, if the comments of Tom Adler and college board members were correct. Maybe it was Ollie's way to avoid conflict. To win friends.

Po frowned. She looked again at her pad. Ollie's name. Joe's. And Halley's added to the chain. Halley had wanted something from Joe's apartment. But there was little there. Writings of Ollie's? But why? Sentimental reasons? Something more, maybe. Something about the house. Revised wills? Notes of intent? Did Halley know something about Ollie that might help find his murderer? As much as she didn't want to distrust Halley, she agreed with Kate that there was something odd about it all.

Po hadn't had the chance she was looking for to talk with Halley. Perhaps tomorrow. She could come over and look through the things from Joe's apartment. There was a picture she knew she would like. Halley and Ollie out beside the pond. Po wondered if Joe had taken it. Such an odd, unlikely threesome.

The darkness outside her window drew Po's attention and she looked over at the clock above her stove. It was late. Max would be there soon to pick her up.

But first she'd call Halley. Po opened a kitchen drawer and paged through the phone directory until she found Halley's name. She dialed it quickly, got an answering machine, and left a brief message. She had found something that Halley might like, she said.

Po hung up and hurried upstairs to dress. The message would bring Halley to her door, she thought. And then they could talk. Po suspected Halley had answers that she didn't even know the questions to.

CHAPTER 23

Po, Max, and Eleanor arrived at Picasso's early, before the usual Friday night crowd. "The better to hear you, my dears," Eleanor said, confessing that the din in restaurants was beginning to bother her eighty-three-year-old ears.

Max laughed. "El, you're amazing. I've been bothered by loud noises for years, and it's just beginning to get to you. What's your secret?"

"Picasso's escargot. One plate a day keeps everything working just fine." She smiled up into the round face of the restaurant owner. "And how are you, dear Picasso?"

Murder on a Starry Night

Picasso St. Pierre bent over and kissed Eleanor on each cheek, then repeated his European ritual with Po. "Beautiful ladies, you honor me tonight with your presence."

"Oh, shush, Picasso," Po said, waving her hand in the air. "You say that to all the women."

"But never with such passion, dear Po," Picasso said, his clear blue eyes twinkling. "That I reserve only for you, mon amie."

"It looks like we're not the only ones coming in early," Max observed, looking around the nearly filled restaurant. Picasso nodded. "Business is good tonight, but not so good other nights. Bad vibrations from the Harrington House. We all feel it, Max."

Max nodded. "I know, Picasso. It's a bad thing."

"But maybe it is solved tonight."

"Oh? What do you mean, Picasso?" Po pushed her glasses up into her hair.

"Monsignor Adler—he was around here earlier—out on the sidewalk. Drunk as a skunk, as you say here. Shouting awful things at Madame Harrington."

"Adele? She was here?"

"Yes, she was here in my restaurant, her ankle bandaged and swollen, but her face quite beautiful. She came in for dinner on the arm of Professor Fellers. A magnificent looking couple, those two."

"Jed Fellers and Adele?" Po's brows lifted.

Max frowned. "That's odd. Jed told me Adele doesn't give him the time of day, and I've seen her be rude to him. Because of Ollie, Jed continues to offer his help to her—he thinks it's what Ollie would have wanted. But Adele is still keeping him at arm's length."

"Maybe she changed her mind," Eleanor said.

"Well, I think it's good that she's getting out," Po said. "And kind of Jed to offer friendship. Was Halley Peterson with them, too?"

Picasso shook his head. "Non. Just the two of them. They had drinks, then my escargot. The professor was gentlemanly and gracious, but he was a little uncomfortable, I think. Not quite himself. And then that awful man began banging on the window, threatening Miss Harrington if she didn't sell him her house. Professor Jed shielded her, moved her away from the window. And then police finally came and took him away. It was frightening my customers. And Miss Harrington was clearly upset at the public display."

"What happened then?" Eleanor asked.

"Miss Harrington insisted they leave. I told her you were coming, Po, maybe she would want to stay and tell you hello. I thought it might calm her down, and I did not want her leaving my restaurant upset. The professor agreed with me. But she wouldn't stay—just grabbed his arm and repeated that she wanted to leave. It wasn't working out as she planned, she said. Professor Fellers told me not to worry. He said he'd take her home, make sure she was okay. But before she left, she did tell me she liked my escargot." Picasso beamed. "She usually does not pay compliments, non?"

Po smiled. No, Adele didn't used to be gracious in that

way. But Adele was making progress, and not just in walking on a swollen ankle.

"But," Picasso continued, pleased with such an attentive audience, "I think with Tom Adler in jail, people might begin to feel better."

"But disturbing the peace isn't proof of murder," Po said.

"Non, you are right, mon amie. But where there is such horrible anger, who knows what more the gendarmes will find?" Picasso took their order for escargots and a ragout d'agneau that, he assured them effusively, would please even his own dear diseased mother, were she here to try it. And in a blink, he scurried off to charm a new group of diners settling in at a nearby table.

"I almost wish Picasso was right about Tom Adler," Po said.

"But he's not," Eleanor added. "Tom Adler is a fool, but not a murderer."

"But he's a desperate fool. Desperation can lead a man to do unexpected things. His wife is a demanding one, that I've seen close-up." Max hailed a waiter and ordered a bottle of white wine.

"Do you really think Tom could be responsible?" Po frowned.

"Po, greed and love are a volatile mix."

"That would explain Ollie's murder, maybe, if he thought he could really get the house if Ollie died. But not Joe."

"Maybe Joe knew something? Maybe witnessed the murder or saw Tom leaving the house that night," Eleanor offered. "And hurting Adele's dog and the fire might have been scare tactics to get Adele to give up her plan for the bed and breakfast."

The waiter silently uncorked a bottle of pinot gris and offered the glass to Max to taste.

"Wonderful," Max assured him, swirling and sniffing the crisp French wine.

"I agree—it all seems plausible," Po said.

"But doesn't settle nicely in the heart, right?" Max looked over at Eleanor and lifted his glass in the air. "To the birthday girl," he said.

Eleanor and Po clinked their glasses together.

"Happy birthday, dear Eleanor." Po sipped her wine and smiled at her friend of so many years that she could no longer keep track.

And with the warm sentiments of birthday and friendship, and the delicious aroma of garlic and butter swirling up from the escargot the waiter placed in front of them, the small group moved on to more appropriate conversation, like Eleanor's planned trip to Southern France.

Later, when they were stuffed full of Picasso's wine-flavored lamb stew, Eleanor, Po, and Max left the restaurant and walked slowly down Elderberry Road. Po linked her arms through Max's and Eleanor's and tilted her head back to look up at the night sky. It was black and beautiful, filled with a sparkling wash of constellations and galaxies. "Amazing," she murmured, her thoughts turning automatically to Oliver Harrington. He was never far from her thoughts these days, and she wondered when he would release his hold on her. When the murderer is found, her mind answered back. That's when.

Po sorted through her thoughts, trying to untangle the threads and wishing the unsettling thoughts would leave her, move on and let her be. She kept returning to Joe's tiny apartment, the life he lived there. And the awareness that the Harrington estate was his whole world. One he rarely left. Except through death. Who could have wanted him dead, a man who had no connections?

Po looked up into the brightly lit window of Gus's bookstore. Eleanor and Max stood before it, examining his new display. "I think I'll see what new travel books Gus has gotten in," Eleanor said.

Po followed them into the store, grappling with one strand of thought that dangled like an irritating thread right in front of her.

The store was crowded with people, some passing the time while they waited for a table at Picasso's, others wandering through the store, listening to a guitarist playing in a reading room or checking out the best sellers on a display rack.

"Gus," Po said, spotting her friend standing in the doorway, talking with a customer.

"Po, about time you wandered over to say hello." Gus stepped closer and gave Po a hug.

It wasn't until Gus's customer turned around that Po realized who it was. "Jed!" she said. "What are you doing here?"

Jed's lip turned up in a half smile. "Talking to Gus?" he asked, confused at her tone.

"Shame on me!" Po said. "That sounded rude. I'm not accustomed to questioning friends' whereabouts, Jed, but Picasso said you were with Adele, so I didn't expect to see you here. And Picasso mentioned the unfortunate encounter at his restaurant tonight."

Jed shoved his hands in his pockets and looked down at Po. "It was unpleasant, Po, that's for sure. Adele isn't the most gracious person in town, but Adler's attack on her was pretty bad. I don't know what the guy was thinking. Too much wine, I guess."

"It was nice of you to take her out, though. I don't think she has left that house at night since she came to town."

"Out?" Jed started to answer, then held his silence.

"Well, Adele gets what she wants, don't you know?" Gus said, stepping into the conversation.

"And what does that mean, Gus?" Po asked.

"Not that there's anything wrong with women asking men out, Po. My Rita says it's done all the time with the college crowd and makes good sense, she says."

"Gus, sometimes you talk too much," Jed said lightly.

"Not at all," Gus retorted. "Everyone in the store heard her invite you to take her to dinner." Gus lowered his voice. "And just between us, we were all pretty relieved it was you she asked out and not any of us."

"Well, I ask Max to take me out all the time," Po said. "You're just too old fashioned, Gus." She smiled at the two men. The news that Adele had initiated the dinner brought an unexpected feeling of relief to Po, and she wasn't at all sure why. Perhaps it was the look on Halley's face when she spotted Jed this morning. Seeing Jed with a woman Halley so disliked would surely have disturbed that smile.

"Adele was in an ornery mood by the time I got her back to her house," Jed said. "I think she was wondering why she'd asked me in the first place. And frankly, I was wondering the same thing. She said she wanted to talk with me about something, but we never got that far. I was fine with making it a short evening, though. I'd promised Halley I'd stop by her place, but when I got there, she wasn't home. I checked out a couple places, then thought maybe I'd find her here. She comes in here a lot. Have either of you seen her?"

"She hasn't been here tonight, Jed," Gus said, but before the words had settled in between them, Po spotted Halley coming in the front door.

Po waved to her over the heads of several customers. "Over here, Halley," she called out.

Halley waved back and wound her way through the crowd to Po's side. When she spotted Jed, she stopped short.

"Hi, Halley" Jed said. "I've been looking for you."

But Halley brushed his hand from her arm and took a step back.

Po frowned. Halley's behavior had been so erratic today. Tonight she seemed highly agitated. Her cheeks were flushed and her eyes darted from Po to Jed, then back to Po. Her face was filled with anger.

"Halley, dear—are you all right?" Po asked.

"I'm fine, Po," Halley snapped. She looked at Jed, a pinched look on her face.

"I got caught up in something, Halley," Jed said. "I'm sorry. Adele—"

"Don't," Halley interrupted. Her tone was sharp, accusing. "Don't talk about her to me."

"Halley," Jed tried again.

Halley held up one hand to stop his words. She looked at Po and opened her mouth as if to speak, then snapped it shut again, her lips pressed into a thin line.

And before Po could say anything to ease the moment, Halley spun around and walked toward the door, her steps angry and heavy on the wooden floor.

Jed looked at Po, started to say something, and then instead, he excused himself and hurried after Halley.

Po was stunned. This wasn't the gentle librarian she had gotten to know in recent weeks. Jealousy certainly wasn't an emotion she'd have suspected would come easily to Halley. Nor disallowing an explanation that could so easily have eased the moment.

Max came up behind her. "Now what was that all about? Halley looked like she was about to kill someone."

Po shook her head. "She was upset, that was for sure. Perhaps Jed will be able to calm her down. He was clearly concerned."

"He has a job on his hands, far as I could tell," Gus said. "You know what they say about a woman scorned—"

"But she wasn't scorned, Gus."

"You know that and I know that, but Halley sure doesn't."

"I'm sure Jed will work it out. The man's a peace maker," Max said beside her.

"There was such anger there," said Po. "But you're right of course. Sometimes all it takes is a good night's sleep. Which is what we all need. Now where in this jungle of books is Eleanor?"

By the time Max and Po found her, Eleanor had discovered several new travel books to buy, and Gus was about to lock his doors.

"Nothing for you, Po?" Gus asked, as they gathered at the checkout desk. "It's a rare day that you leave my store empty-handed. How about a little support for the professor?" He pointed to a small stack of Jed's astronomy books sitting next to the computer. "Someone asked me to order one, so I got a couple extra. Read part of it myself. I think you'll like it."

Eleanor picked up the book and added it to her stack. "My treat," she said.

"Now out, my friends," Gus demanded, returning Eleanor's credit card and handing her the bag. "I need to get home to Rita or she'll wonder what I'm up to."

"And we've had enough of that sort of thing for one night," Max said. "Let's keep the peace at all costs."

Gus laughed and held the door open for then, then locked it behind them.

Keep the peace, Po thought. But she felt anything but peaceful. And even the starry night and two dear friends beside her couldn't shake the feeling that peace was not the operative word tonight.

CHAPTER 24

Max dropped Eleanor off, and he and Po drove in comfortable silence the short distance to Po's home.

Max turned into the driveway, his headlights beaming into the black night in front of them. "Is that Hoover?" he asked, spotting movement beside the back door.

Po frowned. She had left Hoover inside when Max picked her up. But as the car pulled to a stop, Hoover emerged from the shadow of the garage, his tail wagging in recognition. Before Po could get out of the car, he was at her side.

"Hoover, what are you doing out here?" she asked, then

looked over at Max. "That's odd. But sometimes Pete Arango, that nice fellow who mows my lawn, comes over and takes him for a walk. Maybe he didn't latch the door tightly."

"Po, you and your open doors. Will I ever convince you that your open-door policy isn't a great idea?" Max got out and walked around the side of the car.

Po half listened to Max's familiar speech about safety while she scratched Hoover's ears. She'd have to talk to Pete about this. Although Hoover wouldn't venture far, it would only take one squirrel to send him flying across the street—and he wouldn't look both ways first.

Max walked Po to the side door, Hoover close behind, and held it open for her.

"I'd ask you in, Max, but I know you're as tired as I am," Po said.

Max nodded. "And I've an early appointment with a client tomorrow." He held her for a moment, then felt the nudge of Hoover's furry head between them. Max pulled apart slightly, then kissed Po good night. "I think Hoover's tired, too. Who knows what adventures he has had tonight. 'Night big fella," he said, scratching the dog's head, then headed back to his car.

Po watched Max drive away, wondering how she had been so lucky to have, not one, but two amazing men in her life. "And you're not so bad yourself," she said to Hoover, opening the back door and stepping into the low light of the kitchen.

Hoover ran around her, then stopped short, barking loudly into the semi-dark house.

Po's heart began to beat wildly. Something didn't feel right; clearly, Hoover thought so, too.

Hoover raced through the family room and into the front hall, his golden coat flying in the breeze.

"Is someone there?" Po called out, then grabbed a portable phone from the counter, ready to dial 911.

From the front of the house, Hoover barked wildly. Po peered into the darkened front hallway, the phone clenched tightly in her hand, her finger just above the programmed key that would bring the police.

Hoover stood at the front door, his ears alert, his nose pressed against the glass. All was silent, save for the beating of her heart and Hoover's panting.

Po walked cautiously to the door and looked out into the dark night. The solid inner door was pushed wide open. Po stood at the glass storm door behind Hoover, peering out into the darkness. Nothing but the dark, starry night. But someone had been here. Someone had been in her house.

Po shuddered and rubbed her arms. The feeling of being assaulted, of someone invading her private space was as real and poignant as it would have been if she had encountered a trespasser face to face. Po walked through the house quickly, flicking on every switch until the house was ablaze in light and the frantic beating of her heart had slowed.

The fear had dried Po's mouth and she poured a drink of water from the cooler, then stood by the kitchen table, looking around the large living area. Everything looked the same as when she had left the house hours earlier.

Beside her, Hoover began to sniff the floor, then sniffed his way back into the wood-paneled den near the front door.

Po followed slowly, wishing she had asked Max to come inside with her. She turned on the overhead light in the den. Sam's massive old desk was where it always was. But all around it were pieces of paper, tossed about in disarray. The desk drawers were open, and pads of Po's yellow paper had been pulled out and left on the floor beside the desk. Po pressed her hand against her heart and tried to calm the rising fear filling her chest.

The gold clock the college had given Sam on his tenth anniversary as president was still above the mantel. Her laptop computer was still in its rightful place in the middle of the desk. A digital camera sat on a table and CDs filled a bookcase in easy view. Clearly whoever rummaged through her drawers was not out to steal electronics.

Po had brought the pictures salvaged from Joe's apartment upstairs and put them on the table in the den, ready to reframe and return to Adele. Several were on the floor, but as far as she could tell, they all seemed to be there, though rearranged and turned upside down. Po walked back through the hallway and into the family room and kitchen.

There were no signs of anyone being in that part of the house, none, except the door of the closet where she kept her quilting supplies was ajar, and there was a slightly open drawer in the kitchen. But she might have done that herself, Po thought. She'd been in a hurry, she remembered—she'd been thinking about Joe and Ollie's murders, about the stash of things in her basement. She glanced over at the counter where she'd tossed the yellow pad she had been doodling on that afternoon.

It wasn't there.

Po frowned. She retraced her steps to the den, then returned to the kitchen. She had had the pad of paper in her hand, she remembered, and then had set it down carelessly on the counter and gone upstairs to shower and dress. She was sure of that. Because she had planned to go into the basement, but ran out of time.

The basement.

Po walked through the back hallway and down the stairs. She flicked the switch and flooded the basement room with light. The remnants of Joe's life were there, still lined up drying, their pages curled from the process. Nothing seemed to be disturbed.

The trespasser hadn't been in the basement. But a new-comer to her house would need time to find the basement. The door was at the end of a hall and was always closed. Perhaps he had been scared off before he got that far. Or maybe he didn't care about the basement. What was in basements—trunks and old furniture? Probably not a robber's treasure trove. She picked up a small, heat-singed book that she had forgotten the day before and carried it upstairs with her to put with things Halley might want.

Po refilled her water glass and sat on the couch, forcing her heartbeat to slow. Finally, with Hoover curled up in a golden heap on his bed beside the couch, Po walked through the house and locked her doors for the first time since she could remember.

Po poured herself a glass of wine and carried it upstairs. She considered calling the police, but there didn't seem to be anything missing. What could they do? Instead she picked up the new book Eleanor had bought for her and headed up the stairs to bed.

A soak in a hot bath, the glass of wine, and a few chapters of the book relaxed her weary body, and when Po turned out the light a short while, sleep, though fitful, finally came.

CHAPTER 25

"Po, I can't believe you didn't call the police," Selma said, her eyes blazing.

Po had considered skipping the Saturday morning quilting session, but the Bees were nearly finished with all their quilt tops for Adele's bed and breakfast, and Po knew her absence would cause more fuss than sharing her news about last night's break-in with Selma. Now she wasn't so sure.

"Selma, calm down. Nothing was taken. Everything is fine."

"Fine, my foot." Selma walked around the end of the

Murder on a Starry Night

table and plugged in the iron. Her brown clogs pounded on the hardwood floor.

"Have you talked to P.J., Po?" Kate asked.

Po saw the worry fill Kate's enormous brown eyes, and she reached over and patted her hand. "Katie, don't worry about this."

Kate didn't answer. She slipped her hand away and walked over to the sideboard, pouring a cup of coffee and looking out into the Saturday morning, wondering what her life would be like without Po in it.

Eleanor lowered her cane to the floor and sat down next to Po. "Drink this," she said, handing Po a cup of coffee.

"Eleanor, I'm fine."

"Well, I'm not," Eleanor said, "so humor me. If I had my flask, I'd spike it."

Phoebe echoed Eleanor's concern. "Po, it's like this time it wasn't dangerous, but next time? We need to figure this out, stop all this nonsense," Phoebe said. "Why would anyone want to break into your house, Po?"

"That's the first question that needs an answer. You said nothing was taken?" Selma asked. "Doesn't make sense."

"Nothing, except for a yellow pad," Po said. "And most likely I just misplaced that. I doubt if anyone would want my scribblings and grocery lists."

"What was on it?" Maggie asked. Her Fox and Geese quilt top was almost finished and she was as proud of it as she was of her veterinary clinic. She'd pieced the simple design with bright red calico pieces and it would be perfect on the double bed in the corner room at 210 Kingfish Drive.

Leah and Susan walked in from the other room, carrying their already completed quilts. Leah had quilted her own, not trusting it to a second party.

"Gorgeous," Maggie exclaimed as she spied the armful of quilt in Leah's arms. She was up in a flash and took one corner of the quilt from Leah. Together they held it high for the others to see.

For the quilt top, Leah had created her own design, piecing together a bed of rolling hills—strips of bright greens and blues, shades of rust and goldenrod filled the quilt top in uneven waves. And on top of the design, in crimson and yellows and purples, she had appliquéd sunflowers and daisies and black cherry coleus. Brilliant zinnias, their heads full and flowering. Between the appliquéd prairie flowers, she'd woven strands of prairie grasses into the design. It was a contemporary prairie flowerbed, a work of art, and quilted in graceful waves that matched the field—intricate, perfect lines of stitching. For the binding that held the three layers of the quilt together, Leah had found a navy blue fabric, filled with tiny dots of color that matched the flowers.

"Magnificent, Leah. You've outdone yourself," Po said, grateful for the shift in conversation.

"It's going in that large bedroom with the sitting room off to the side," Leah said.

A rattling at the back door broke into the conversation, and Po looked over at P.J.'s lanky frame filling the doorway.

"H'lo ladies," he said with a lopsided grin, not totally comfortable in a roomful of needles and strange tools he didn't understand. He walked over to the sideboard, helping himself to a cinnamon roll.

"Are you taking up quilting, P.J.?" Po asked, wondering when Kate had managed to send him an S.O.S. without Po seeing it.

"Not today, Po." P.J. walked over to her and bent low, his face not far from hers. "Heard you had a visitor last night."

"I guess I did, P.J." Po said. "But he didn't do any damage—"

"He?" P.J. pulled up a chair and straddled it from behind.

"He. She. I don't know the sex, P.J., but whoever it was saw fit to leave without causing much damage."

"Except to your peace of mind," Kate said from her place at the window.

"Yes, that was shaken," Po admitted.

"Any idea who would have come in like that? Or what they wanted?" P.J. asked.

Po had thought of that question since five that morning when she'd tugged on faded sweat pants and a hoodie, and run slowly through the neighborhood, circled around the campus, and finally run all the way down to the river park and back. Who, indeed? She almost wished a camera or computer was missing. That would make it simple. An honest-to-goodness robbery. But as far as she knew, nothing was missing. So it had to be something else. Someone who wanted something she had—and couldn't find it.

"Po?" P.J. said. "If all those thoughts rattling around in your head were spoken words, I think I'd be a giant step further in understanding what went on last night."

Po shook her head. "No, I don't think you would be. It doesn't make any sense at all." But she knew deep down that it *did* make sense, it all made sense somehow—if only her mind could order it correctly. Was it someone she knew? That thought caused the deepest unrest. She could account for those she was with last night, but that was a short list of two. Her emotions fought any possible list she tried to put together. But the truth was, someone had entered house while she was gone. In those few hours, protected by her absence, someone had rifled through her things. Po rubbed her hands up and down her arms and sighed.

Kate bit down on her bottom lip as she listened to the talk around her. She was as sure as she'd ever been of anything in her life that whatever happened at Po's last night was connected to the murders. And that thought caused ripples of fear to travel up her spine.

P.J. walked over and looped an arm around her shoulders, pulling her close. "It's okay, Katie," he whispered into her hair. "We won't let anything happen to Po. If someone had intended to do her harm, they would have come when she was home." And then he looked around at the room filled with women who'd inched their way into his life—Eleanor and Selma with their plain wisdom and humor, the irrepressible Phoebe and quiet, talented Susan. Beautiful, earthy Leah, And down-to-earth Maggie, smart as a whip, with a heart as big as Kansas. He had only been drawn into this unlikely circle of friends because Po and Kate had put him there.

They were strong, independent women, every single one of them. And that was exactly what pulled at his emotions and caused stabs of concern to settle uncomfortably inside him. There was nothing those ladies wouldn't do for one another. Even if it meant putting themselves in the middle of a murder investigation. Even if it meant attacking danger head on and worrying about the consequences later.

CHAPTER 26

When Kate and Po walked out of Selma's store several hours later, the wind was coming from the north, and Po shivered against the unexpected chill. "I'll drive you home, Kate," she said.

Kate nodded. She was shivering, too. But whether from the crisp, sharp air or the recent conversation, she couldn't be sure. P.J. had left earlier with worry in his eyes and his forehead pinched. "Kate," he had started to say as she walked with him to the door, but Kate quieted him with two fingers pressed against his lips.

"Shhh," she had said, "We aren't foolish, P.J."

But after P.J. had left the shop, the quilters' conversation grew animated and emotional. "There is no way on God's earth that a regular old thief would wander into Po's home, then decide to leave without taking things. This is connected to Ollie and Joe's murder, as sure as anything," Eleanor declared.

And Phoebe had stood up at the end of the table and declared that it was time to get serious.

"And find out why someone would want both Ollie and Joe dead," Eleanor had finished.

"And if you want to know what I think," Phoebe had concluded, her arms folded across her chest and her eyes clear and wide. "I don't think it has a thing to do with building condominiums at 210 Kingfish Drive."

"Po, I think Phoebe is right," Kate said now, climbing into Po's CRV. She snapped her seatbelt in place. "These deaths aren't about that house. Joe and Ollie knew something someone didn't want them to know."

"I think so, too, Kate."

"So it's more personal, more intimate."

Po nodded. She turned onto Kate's street and pulled into the driveway of the small house that Kate's parents had left to their only child. It was a cozy bungalow, and Kate's parents had refinished it to its original shine, restoring the dark wood molding and filling it with Stickley furniture in the original arts and crafts style. Po had spent many hours on the wide front porch with Liz, Kate's mom. Sitting, gossiping, comforting, enlightening. All the things best friends do.Sometimes they'd laugh about how safe their houses made them feel. And today, Po thought, this house felt far more safe than her own.

"Are you listening to me, Po?" Kate asked, undoing her seat belt and shifting on the seat to stare at Po. "You're not hearing me."

Po forced a smile. "Of course I am, Kate. I have a lot on my mind today, I guess."

"Po, P.J. will pass everything along to those working on the case."

"I know that, Kate."

"And they will find whoever did this."

Po reached over and gave Kate a hug. "Yes," she said. And they'd find out that it might have been right in front of them all along. And that thought had tugged at her all morning, as pieces finally began to fall into place. One had to think outside the box, she thought. However disturbing and difficult that might be.

From Kate's, Po drove directly to Canterbury University, hoping that the library would be very quiet on a Saturday afternoon. It was not a trip she wanted to make, but she needed to talk with Halley. Her behavior at the bookstore had been strange. And where was Halley before that, when someone was wandering around Po's house without an invitation?

Po parked her car and walked up the stairs to the massive stone library, built many years ago by Eleanor's grandfather. When she walked through the turnstyle, she spotted Halley immediately, standing behind the resource desk working on a computer. She looks sad, Po thought, as she made her way around a book display. The range of emotions the woman had displayed in just a few days was remarkable, Po thought. Joy, anger, jealousy, sadness. What would be next?

"Halley?" Po said.

Halley's head jerked up. Her face was drawn, and she seemed, at first, to not recognize Po.

Po stood there, silent, waiting for Halley to step in, to fill in some of the cavernous cracks.

Finally, Halley collected herself. "I'm rather busy, if you've come to see me." Her voice was formal and cool.

"Is everything all right, Halley?"

Halley managed a smile. "Of course."

"Did you get my message about the things I'd found at Joe's?"

Halley nodded. "Thank you. I came by last night— but you weren't home."

"And did you find it?"

Halley looked puzzled. "Find what?"

"The things you were looking for at Joe's apartment."

"Of course not," Halley snapped. "Are you saying I went inside your house?"

"Kate and the others sometimes just go right in and make themselves at home."

"Maybe they would. I wouldn't do that." Halley played with a strand of hair that had fallen across her cheek, twisting it into a spiral. She stared at Po, challenging her,

her chest moving in and out as she tried to control herself.

"Did you tell anyone else about Joe's things?"

"Of course not. Why would anyone else care?"

"No matter. I'm going to look through some of Joe's things later today—and if you'd like, you're welcome to see what's there. There's a photo of you and Ollie that you might like. Perhaps I'll find some other things in the meantime."

Halley face was expressionless. She nodded.

An awkward silence filled the space between them.

"Well, then," Po said, "Perhaps I'll see you later."

Halley nodded and looked down. Her fingers began frantically punching keys on the computer, dismissing Po. Her face was grim.

Po paused for a moment, then rummaged in her purse for her car keys. Her fingers touched the small book she had found at Joe's and dropped in her purse. Impulsively, she pulled it out and set it on the library counter. "Here, Halley. Take this. It's from Joe's and perhaps belonged to Ollie." Then she forced a smile to her face, turned and walked out of the library, feeling Halley's eyes on her back as she walked through the wide front door.

In the car Po tried to process Halley Peterson's behavior. Had she totally misread this young woman? Though Po had seen Halley's anger when she talked about Adele Harrington—and in Gus's bookstore more recently—the frosty façade she presented to Po today was something new. But if Halley was trying to rebuff Po, she was choosing the wrong tactic. If nothing else, her behavior only added to Po's resolve to talk with her.

Po's next stop was the Harrington mansion, and she found Adele walking in the back gardens, looking relaxed, in spite of the still-swollen ankle that kept her pace slow and measured.

Adele smiled at Po as she approached. "What a nice surprise, Po. What brings you here today?"

"I thought I'd give you a quilt update," Po said. She fell in step beside her. "Susan and Leah have finished theirs, and the rest are nearly ready to go. I think you're going to love them."

"I've no doubt, Po. I hired the best."

Po smiled. "I wanted you to know that I'm drying out some of Ollie's things that I found at Joe's. Some pictures. Some writings of his. He was quite good, people tell me."

"Oh, he was a lovely writer, even when he was young. I sent him a computer once—but he hated it. He said his fingers needed the feel of the pen in them, that his thoughts worked themselves down from his head, through his fingers and the pencil to paper. The computer messed up the route."

Po laughed. "I thought that way once, but forced myself to get used to it. And of course it became my good friend. But I understand what Ollie was saying. So he always wrote in longhand?"

"Always." Adele looked off toward the pond. "I found a bunch of yellow pads in his room, filled from top to bottom with his familiar scrawl. But I couldn't quite get myself to read them. I found Joe up in his room shortly after Ollie died, going through them. He wanted them so badly, that

I gave in." She frowned. "It was odd, now that I think back. He was very peculiar that day, muttering that it would be better for me if he had them. But he was such a strange little man, that I guess I didn't pay much attention."

Po listened carefully to Adele. "If find anything in the things I've taken home, I will save it for you. It would be good for you to have some of Ollie's things."

"Yes. I've reached the point, I think, where I can talk to people who knew Ollie. For a while, it made me feel guilty, that people like Joe and Halley Peterson and Jed Fellers knew Ollie better than I did. Even Tom Adler spent more time with him in recent months. And Ollie liked them all. I'm not so fond of some of them, but I've decided that keeping them all at bay is rather foolish of me because they knew a part of Ollie I would like to know better. And so I shall not be so standoffish. In fact, for starters, I intended to talk with Jed Fellers about building a small observatory in Ollie's honor. He seems to know a lot about that sort of thing and Ollie certainly loved it."

"That's a lovely thought, Adele," Po said. "I imagine Jed thought so too."

"Well, my discussion with him was interrupted," Adele said. "We didn't quite get around to it. Later, perhaps."

"That was your dinner at Picasso's?" Halley Peterson's jealousy was most definitely misplaced, Po thought.

"Yes. There are no secrets in this town, are there? You heard about the episode, of course."

Po nodded. "Picasso told us. He was concerned. And I am, too. You need to be careful, Adele." Careful and

Murder on a Starry Night

judicious, Po thought. Adele was so close to the dreadful things going on. Po wondered if she gave that fact proper attention. And she was wrong about one thing—there were plenty of secrets in this town. Perhaps dangerous ones.

"Don't worry Po," Adele said, seeing the concern in Po's eyes. "It will take more than a drunk to frighten me away. He has a demanding wife, that's all."

"But when people drink too much, you don't know what they are capable of."

"Some people are more dangerous when they are sober, Po. But don't worry. If I am anything, I am cautious."

"Adele," Po said suddenly, "Why did you leave Crestwood the way you did, and not return?"

"I left for college," Adele said. It was a pat, no nonsense answer, without the personal touch of their earlier conversation.

"But after that, when Ollie came home. You didn't seem to be around much. Perhaps I am treading on personal ground, and please tell me if I am. But did you not get along with your mother?"

"Oh my, is that what people thought?" Adele sat down on a stone bench near a garden of mums and looked off over the yard. "I loved my mother, though we disagreed about a lot. Ollie, mainly. She babied him too much. Protected him so severely because of his learning disabilities that when she got sick, she made Joe Bates promise to stay here forever because Ollie had never lived alone."

"Why didn't she want you to be that person?"

For a long time Adele didn't answer, but Po could see the years passing across her mind. Sadness and happiness, pain and joy flashed from her eyes as the memories rolled. Finally she answered the question Po had posed. "It was my father whom I disliked. Intensely. He was not a good man, at least not in all respects. His affairs during mother's pregnancies—she lost three babies—were cruel, but when he bedded a friend of mine on a college break, then threatened me later if I said a word, it became too much. And my mother urged me to leave this town and make a life for myself away from it all. She used to come and see me every chance she got—she was a good person. But she needed the money Walter Harrington provided. She needed it for Ollie.

"My father never cared for Ollie. Broken, was the word he used. I, the healthy twin, survived. Ollie was weakened. An accident, my father said, and he made it clear to me that I should have been the one. Not Ollie. Not the boy.

"But Walter Harrington did genuinely worship my mother, in spite of all his transgressions. And when she laid down the rules, he complied, leaving her and Ollie to live their life as mother saw fit." Adele rose from the bench and began walking back toward the house. Po fell in beside her.

"We weren't exactly the Cleaver family, were we? But we survived. And I think my mother did the best she could. But even knowing that, I resented what this town, this house, stood for, for a long time. But when

Murder on a Starry Night

Ollie died, I decided I'd at least give it a try—try to make peace with some of the demons."

"And I think you have," Po said. "Or are on your way."

"Not yet. Not completely. As long as there are still people out there who think I murdered my brother, I can never really fit in here, can I?"

The sad plea from the strong, implacable Adele Harrington touched Po in a way that made her shiver in the cool fall air. She pulled her wool sweater closed and buttoned it. "Adele," she said, touching her arm lightly, "Hang in a little bit longer. I think that will end soon." And for better or worse, Po knew her words to be true.

CHAPTER 27

Po pulled out of Adele's driveway and headed home.
This time she wouldn't be distracted. She would go through
every single piece of paper, every picture she had taken from
Joe Bates' apartment. And she'd find the answers to all her
questions, she was sure of it. At the least, she'd get closer
to the ties that bound Ollie Harrington to the few people
he allowed in his life each day.

She thought back to her brief conversation with Adele.
Why was Joe Bates so insistent that he get Ollie's musings?
What had Ollie written that was so important to someone

like Joe Bates, someone who didn't even like to read? Joe wasn't sentimental, that much she knew about him. But he loved Ollie Harrington. And Ollie's murder had turned him into a mumbling old man, a man determined, perhaps, to bring his murderer to light. That would have been Joe's goal. Of course it would.

And stuck in his desk and apartment were legal papers, notes from Ollie, and heaven knows what else. The gatherings of a man determined to right a terrible wrong.

Po punched in Gus Schuette's phone number on her cell. "Gus," she said quickly, knowing he probably had a store full of Saturday shoppers. "Gus, you mentioned recently that Joe Bates had come into your store shortly before he was killed. Joe wasn't much of a reader. What was he buying?"

As busy as his store was, Gus liked to chat, and Po waited patiently while he confirmed that Joe didn't seem to read much, but he sure loved Gus's garden magazines when he used to come in the store more often. But that day—Gus remembered it clearly, he said, because it was shortly after Ollie's murder, and Joe was a broken man. He'd shuffled into the store, made his purchase, and shuffled out, head down, face a mask of sad anger. He'd picked up a book Gus had ordered for him. Not a garden book at all.

Gus didn't need to finish.

Po knew. It made sense now, what she should have figured out weeks ago. She drove into her driveway, scattering leaves in all directions. Around her, night began to settle in. Po turned off the ignition and slid quickly out of the car. The box with Ollie's yellow pads was still in the back of her car, a safer spot than her house these days, she'd decided. She pulled it out and carried it through the back door, into the soft lights of her kitchen.

Po glanced at the phone and saw that the message light was blinking. She set the box in the den, returned to the kitchen and punched the machine button. The voice was tight and controlled. "Po," it said, "This is Halley Peterson. Perhaps you and I need to have a talk."

Po shivered. *No, not yet*, she said to herself.

Po switched on more lights, then turned her radio to a Saturday jazz concert. The mellow strains of an old Miles Davis rendition of *Summertime* filled the room. Po found odd comfort in the clear trumpet sounds, but she knew it would take more than music to get rid of the chill in her bones. She needed Max, someone else in her home.

A quick call to his home went unanswered. Po tried Kate, but when she got the answering machine, she realized she didn't want Kate around anyway, not tonight, and she left a mundane message instead.

Minutes later, with a large mug cradled in her hands and the smell of orange and spices wafting up from the steaming tea, Po sat down at Sam's big desk, and went to work. "Sam, help me here," she whispered. "Let's get this over with, however sad and distasteful a task it may be." Po pulled out Ollie Harrington's yellow pads and began to read.

The pieces flowed together seamlessly, as they often did when the most obvious situations suddenly came into focus. The only questions remaining would have to come from someone else.

Po shoved the papers into an old portfolio of Sam's and snapped it shut. Another call to Max confirmed that he wasn't in yet, and Po knew she couldn't wait any longer. It needed to end tonight.

Po returned to the kitchen and thumbed through the phone book until she found the address. And then, with her heart in her throat, Po grabbed the portfolio, her purse and a jacket and headed into the dark night. She paused briefly before sliding into her car and looked up into the sky. Millions of stars were flung across a deep velvet blanket. A perfect starry night.

As Po drove down the street, she called Max again from her cell phone, but he didn't pick up, and she remembered a late meeting he'd had. He would be over later, he had told her earlier in the day. Po thought about waiting for him, then decided to forge ahead. The sooner she got all the answers, the better for everyone.

Po pulled out the address and drove slowly through the neighborhood just to the east of campus. It was a pleasant one, with modest houses and new condominiums mixed together. The address was in a small, pleasant complex of town homes, and Po found 707 Elm Street easily enough. There was a light in the window, and Po sat in her car for a brief moment, then walked up the short walkway and rang the bell.

"Hello, Halley," she said.

———

Kate finally reached Max as he was leaving his restaurant meeting. "Please come, Max. I think Po needs us."

The frantic edge to Kate's voice startled Max. Before he could respond, Kate rushed on.

"She left me a message in an odd voice. She asked me to bring pie to dinner tomorrow night."

"I don't get it, Kate."

"Max," Kate said, exasperated with the sometimes slowness of such a smart man. "Po makes pie, not me. She's famous for apple pie. I've never made a piecrust in my life that didn't end up being used as a doorstop. Something's wrong."

Max didn't argue. Po had left him a message, too— she said she was going to Halley's. She also needed him to stand by her, she'd said. There's no place he'd rather stand. Without hesitation, Max walked quickly out of the office and headed for his car.

"Come in," Halley said. Her face matched her white tee shirt except for red, bleary eyes.

Po followed Halley into the small living room and sat down across from her. "It's time you told me the truth, Halley."

Halley nodded, but when she began to talk, the tears started again. She grabbed a tissue from the nearly empty container and looked steadily at Po. "I don't know where to start, Po, but first you need to know I adored Ollie.

Sincerely." Po nodded. She had responses to that—that Halley had a peculiar way of expressing it—but she held her silence, waiting for the answers she was seeking.

"I didn't know what Ollie had written, Po. Joe never told me. Jed and I wanted them back, because he said maybe we could publish them, honor Ollie in a special way. A book of essays, maybe. And Jed said Adele would never do that. But I knew it was what Ollie would want. He always wanted to write a book. So I tried hard to get them, to do something decent for him."

"And you tried to break into Joe's after he died—"

"I knew Joe had them. He told me that day that he needed to talk to me. That it was a matter of life and death. After he died, I thought it was in the writings."

"Why didn't you tell anyone?"

"Jed was helping me. He encouraged me to get them."

"And when you knew I had them?"

"I lied to you that day, Po. I was so upset. I loved him, you know."

"Jed?"

She nodded and the tears began to flow. "I told Jed you had some things for me from Joe's, and when I drove by that night, I saw him going into your house. I confronted him later and he said he was getting some keys he'd left in your kitchen. When you want desperately to believe someone, lies can be easily masked.

"But I didn't trust him completely, and I was so angry and sad. I felt used and I hated myself for it. And then you kept after me with questions. I just wanted everyone to leave me alone until I could get through it all and figure out what to do."

Halley looked up at Po and her eyes were filled with grief. "Jed was the first love of my life, Po. I'm thirty-six, and he was my first love. I didn't know what to do about that, don't you see?"

"You wanted to hang on to it if you could. I understand, Halley."

"Jed wouldn't give me a copy of his book, you know. He said he was embarrassed by his first effort, and I could read the next one. I was so foolish. Even though I thought it was odd, I did what he asked. But when you left it with me, I paged through it and knew what I guess I'd known for awhile—knew that I had heard those beautiful, lyrical words before. Ollie used to read the passages to me after he'd written them. I'd sit in wonder, imagining the stars he wrote about, the pathways and galaxies and amazing dimensions of the universe."

"So it was Ollie, then, who wrote *A Plain Man's Guide to a Starry Night.*"

Po was talking more to herself than to Halley.

"Yes."

Halley spun around at the sound of the familiar voice behind her.

Jed walked into the low light of the living room and dropped Halley's house key on the table. He walked over to Halley and rested one arm on her hand.

"Halley, I love you. And I'll explain all of this." He looked over at Po and asked her politely to sit down.

Po saw the bulge in Jed's coat pocket, and she sat down on the edge of the couch. His voice was dangerously calm. He kept his hand on Halley's arm and continued, his eyes never leaving Po's face.

"It's too bad that you pursued this to such lengths, Po. We'd all be better off—you, me, Halley—if you had left it alone."

"But Ollie and Joe weren't left alone, Jed."

"I didn't want it to end like it did. I'm not a monster, Po." Jed half-smiled as he spoke, and Po felt chills run down her back.

"Ollie wrote those essays in my class, you know. Shared them all with me. They were brilliant, so I photocopied each one. All I had to do was add a transition here and there and a title. It all made a kind of logical sense to me. I was his mentor, after all.

"I called Ollie into my office when the publisher sent me a copy of the book," Jed continued calmly, "and I told him what a great thing it was—he was a published author, wasn't that great? I explained that it didn't matter whose name was on it, he was the vision behind it, and we'd celebrate together."

Beside him, Halley shook her head. "You're a fool, Jed Fellers. Ollie would never have agreed to that. I could have told you that."

"No, in his simple way, Ollie had a ridiculous sense of right and wrong. Black and white. He said it was dishonest. Against the law. Said he was going to go to the chancellor and tell him. I tried everything I could think of to change his mind. I needed the book, for god's sake. The tenure committee was breathing down my neck. The department chair was at stake. Ollie didn't need it. But I did. When Ollie wouldn't cooperate, I had no choice."

"But to kill him?" Halley screamed at Jed and jerked her arm away.

Jed slapped her. "Halley, calm down," he said. His voice was monotone now and Po recognized the lack of emotion, the distance in his tone, and it frightened her.

"Po, you don't get it because you've always had it easy. You and Sam. You don't know what it's like."

Jed's tone was changing dramatically, and Po stiffened. "You killed a lovely man, Jed. And you stole from him."

"Not a theft, Po!" Jed's voice was threatening now. "Who do you think taught Oliver those things? Who?"

"I'm sure you taught him some things, Jed. But you also took his words and told people they were yours. Ollie must have told Joe Bates about it."

"Of course he did. And Joe would have done anything for Ollie. Joe took the original essays after Ollie died, I was sure of it."

"So you tried to burn his place down? It was you, not Halley."

Jed laughed. "Halley? Halley couldn't hurt a flea, but she'd do anything for a friend." His hand moved up to Halley's neck and he tugged lightly on a strand of her hair. "But when Halley couldn't get the notebooks, burning the place seemed the easiest way out."

"And now what, Jed?" Po faced him directly. She'd

known Jed Fellers for over a dozen years. Or she thought she had. But suddenly, she was forced to face a man that she didn't know at all.

Jed stood straight and looked her in the eye. "I don't know, Po. What do you think we should do?" He shrugged and looked at her with total disinterest. "I thought I'd find the manuscripts before you did, and no one would ever have known. But you butted in. And I know one thing, I can't let you destroy my fine reputation." His hand slipped into his pocket.

Beside him, Halley rubbed her arms, then took a step away. A noise from the kitchen distracted Jed for the one brief moment that Halley needed, and while Po watched, she raised her knee, positioned her hand for a chop to his throat, and before Po could get up from the couch, she sent Jed Fellers flying to the floor.

In the next instant, Max, appeared in the doorway, followed by a policeman. He wrapped his arm around Halley. "That was quite a move, young lady."

"I walk home alone from the library nearly every night. A girl has to be ready," she said, and moved over to Po, hugging her tightly.

Outside, lined up along the green lawn beneath a perfect, star-filled sky, stood a collection of Crestwood police, eager for their prey.

And behind them, shivering beneath the folds of P.J.'s down jacket, Kate looked up beyond the stars and thanked her mother once again for looking out for those she loved.

EPILOGUE

You are cordially invited
to Thanksgiving Dinner
210 Kingfish Drive

RSVP — Adele Harrington

Adele had decided Thanksgiving would be the perfect weekend to open the doors of 210 Kingfish Drive to the town that had finally embraced her as one of its own.

With a crew of many and the help of Picasso St. Pierre and his staff at the French Quarter, Adele threw a Thanksgiving dinner that would be remembered and talked about for a long, long time.

"Adele, you've definitely outdone yourself," Po said, walking through the wide welcoming front door with Eleanor and Max on either side of her. "It's absolutely beautiful!"

In the four weeks since the jail doors had banged closed on Jed Fellers, Adele Harrington had thrown herself full force into finishing the renovation of her home in time for the holiday. The knowledge that Ollie's murderer was a man she knew, a man who was so present during all their grieving, was difficult to accept, and work proved an acceptable antidote to the pain.

Dozens of mums in rusts and gold filled the warm, inviting entryway of the home for the special event. Candles warmed tabletops and the soft light of sconces welcomed guests into Crestwood's newest B&B.

Kate walked through the open door on P.J.'s arm. "I want to be married right here, in this amazing place. Can we do that, Adele?" She smiled over at their hostess.

Adele wrapped an arm around Kate and took her over to the staircase, just beyond the small desk where visitors would soon be signing in. "How proud I'd be to have little Kate Simpson be the first bride to come down those stairs. Adele pointed up the massive winding staircase that led to the second level. Thick forest-green carpet lined the stairs, and ropes of garlands lit with tiny white lights, were wound around the walnut railing. A harvest tree decorated the landing.

"Hey, what did I miss?" P.J. said, following the two women. "Wedding? Katie my love, am I invited?"

Po watched P.J. follow Kate up the stairs to tour the renovated bedroom suites. A wedding at 210 Kingfish Drive? The thought filled her with a rush of dizzying warmth.

"You're wearing your heart on your lovely sleeve, Po," Max whispered in her ear, then handed her a crystal glass of punch.

Po chuckled and walked on into the spacious living room where Selma and Susan were sitting on a couch in front of the blazing fire. Gus and Rita Schuette were off to the side, admiring the built-in bar that Adele would use for evening wine tastings, and the mayor and college chancellor sat watching a football game in a small alcove area off the living room.

"Something for everyone," Po said, looking around.

"This place is amazing," Maggie said, coming up behind Po. "I'm crazy about it, and Adele has already promised me that we can have a fundraiser for the animal rescue league here." Maggie had brought a guest. "The guardian of four gorgeous adopted pups," was how Maggie introduced him, and his bold, strong face and ready laugh told Po he would be a great match for her dear Maggie.

Tim and Leah came in carrying Leah's homemade pumpkin pies, and Po walked back to the kitchen with Tim. "Picasso," she called out, "more pies for your collection."

Picasso swooped down on them, kissing them both and taking the pies over to the sideboard where they joined others of cherry and mincemeat and rich pecan.

"A feast fit for a French pilgrim," he exclaimed with glee. Halley appeared from the back room with Neptune the cat in her arms.

"Halley, I'm so glad you've come," Po said, giving her a quick hug.

"I guess you haven't heard, Po."

"What's that, dear?"

"Adele has hired me to organize the library that she'll have for the guests. It's going to be wonderful, and I'll work here when I'm not needed at the college. It's kind of a dream," she confessed. "I can pick the books I want, organize it, make it cozy and wonderful. I can't imagine the guests will ever want to leave."

Po knew that Adele and Halley had talked, but she didn't know the outcome had been so generous and forgiving on both their parts. They'd each been hurt terribly by a man, and they had both loved another man whom they couldn't bring back to life. They certainly had a framework for friendship, Po thought. She was pleased to see it had begun.

When Adele called them all into the living room a short while later, Po was prepared for a toast. What she wasn't prepared for was the president of Canterbury University's announcement. "There will be a new printing of *A Plain Man's Guide to a Starry Night*," he said, "with Oliver Harrington's name on the cover."

Adele stood beside him, her eyes damp. She wiped the tears aside and took her place in front of the fireplace. "In addition to the book," she said, "there's something else we've decided to do in my brother's memory." She nodded toward P.J. and Max.

The two men walked in from the foyer, carrying a folded mound of fabric. With the Queen Bees standing proudly by, they unfolded and held up a hanging that Susan and Leah had designed, and all the Queen Bees had stitched together in these four short weeks. A gift for Adele. A tribute to Ollie.

The background blocks of mottled midnight blue held a brilliant galaxy, created from small crimson and gold and deep orange-colored strips. The design was a swirl in all shades and hues. The swirl spread out against the deep background, bigger and bigger, flying upward, until the largest star of all—a brilliant blend of bright orange and yellow and white fabric, filled the top of the quilt.

Ollie's starry sky.

While champagne glasses clinked around the room, Po edged in beside Kate and Max. She looped an arm around each of them, her heart about as full as she could ever remember it being. There was a magic in the air tonight, and she suspected she wasn't the only one who felt it. She hugged her goddaughter close and spoke softly.

"A wedding, Kate?" she asked. "Is that what I heard you say? A wedding on a starry night...I think I could handle that just fine. Just fine, indeed."

ABOUT THE AUTHOR

Sally Goldenbaum is the author of over two dozen published novels, including a mystery written with Nancy Pickard. She is an editor at a veterinary publishing company, mother of three grown children, and lives in Prairie Village, Kansas, with her husband, Don, two dogs, and a cat.